Cram101 Textbook Outlines to accompany:

Advertising Campaign Strategy: A Guide to Marketing Communication Plans

Donald Parente, 4th Edition

PRACTICE EXAMS.

Get all of the self-teaching practice exams for each chapter of this textbook at **www.Cram101.com** and ace the tests. Here is an example:

Chapter 1

Advertising Campaign Strategy: A Guide to Marketing Communication Plans
Donald Parente, 4th Edition,
All Material Written and Prepared by Cram101

I WANT A BETTER GRADE. Items 1 - 50 of 100.

1 A _________ strategy targets non-buying customers in currently targeted segments. It also targets new customers in new segments. (Winer)

A marketing manager has to think about the following questions before implementing a _________ strategy: Is it profitable? Will it require the introduction of new or modified products? Is the customer and channel well enough researched and understood?

The marketing manager uses these four groups to give more focus to the market segment decision: existing customers, competitor customers, non-buying in current segments, new segments.

- Market Development
- Maas International
- Machiavellianism
- Machine learning

2 The acronym _________, is a psychographic segmentation. It was developed in the 1970s to explain changing U.S. values and lifestyles. It has since been reworked to enhance its ability to predict consumer behavior.

According to the _________ Framework, groups of people are arranged in a rectangle and are based on two dimensions. The vertical dimension segments people based on the degree to which they are innovative and have resources such as income, education, self-confidence, intelligence, leadership skills, and energy.

- VALS
- Vacation
- Vacheron Constantin
- Vacuum packing

You get a 50% discount for the online exams. Go to **Cram101.com**, click Sign Up at the top of the screen, and enter DK73DW6327 in the promo code box on the registration screen. Access to Cram101.com is $4.95 per month, cancel at any time.

With Cram101.com online, you also have access to extensive reference material.

You will nail those essays and papers. Here is an example from a Cram101 Biology text:

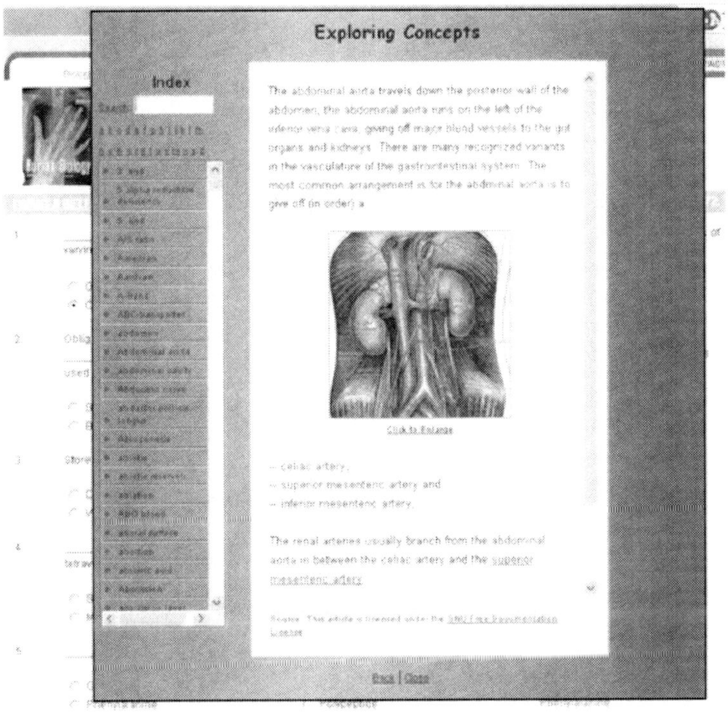

Visit **www.Cram101.com**, click Sign Up at the top of the screen, and enter DK73DW6327 in the promo code box on the registration screen. Access to www.Cram101.com is normally $9.95 per month, but because you have purchased this book, your access fee is only $4.95 per month, cancel at any time. Sign up and stop highlighting textbooks forever.

Learning System

Cram101 Textbook Outlines is a learning system. The notes in this book are the highlights of your textbook, you will never have to highlight a book again.

How to use this book. Take this book to class, it is your notebook for the lecture. The notes and highlights on the left hand side of the pages follow the outline and order of the textbook. All you have to do is follow along while your instructor presents the lecture. Circle the items emphasized in class and add other important information on the right side. With Cram101 Textbook Outlines you'll spend less time writing and more time listening. Learning becomes more efficient.

Cram101.com Online

Increase your studying efficiency by using Cram101.com's practice tests and online reference material. It is the perfect complement to Cram101 Textbook Outlines. Use self-teaching matching tests or simulate in-class testing with comprehensive multiple choice tests, or simply use Cram's true and false tests for quick review. Cram101.com even allows you to enter your in-class notes for an integrated studying format combining the textbook notes with your class notes.

Visit **www.Cram101.com**, click Sign Up at the top of the screen, and enter **DK73DW6327** in the promo code box on the registration screen. Access to www.Cram101.com is normally $9.95 per month, but because you have purchased this book, your access fee is only $4.95 per month. Sign up and stop highlighting textbooks forever.

 ISBN(s): 9781428842373.

Advertising Campaign Strategy: A Guide to Marketing Communication Plans
Donald Parente, 4th

CONTENTS

Market Development	A Market development strategy targets non-buying customers in currently targeted segments. It also targets new customers in new segments. (Winer) A marketing manager has to think about the following questions before implementing a Market development strategy: Is it profitable? Will it require the introduction of new or modified products? Is the customer and channel well enough researched and understood? The marketing manager uses these four groups to give more focus to the market segment decision: existing customers, competitor customers, non-buying in current segments, new segments.
VALS	The acronym VALS, is a psychographic segmentation. It was developed in the 1970s to explain changing U.S. values and lifestyles. It has since been reworked to enhance its ability to predict consumer behavior. According to the VALS Framework, groups of people are arranged in a rectangle and are based on two dimensions. The vertical dimension segments people based on the degree to which they are innovative and have resources such as income, education, self-confidence, intelligence, leadership skills, and energy.
Media Market	A Media market, broadcast market, media region, designated market area (DMA), Television Market Area (FCC term) or simply market is a region where the population can receive the same (or similar) television and radio station offerings, and may also include other types of media including newspapers and Internet content. They can coincide with metropolitan areas, though rural regions with few significant population centers can also be designated as markets. Conversely, very large metropolitan areas can sometimes be subdivided into multiple segments.
Consumer	Consumer is a broad label for any individuals or households that use goods and services generated within the economy. The concept of a Consumer is used in different contexts, so that the usage and significance of the term may vary. Typically when business people and economists talk of Consumers they are talking about person as Consumer, an aggregated commodity item with little individuality other than that expressed in the buy/not-buy decision.
Research	research is defined as human activity based on intellectual application in the investigation of matter. The primary purpose for applied research is discovering, interpreting, and the development of methods and systems for the advancement of human knowledge on a wide variety of scientific matters of our world and the universe. research can use the scientific method, but need not do so.
Survey research	Survey research a research method involving the use of questionnaires and/or statistical surveys to gather data about people and their thoughts and behaviours.
Procter ' Gamble	Procter is a surname, and may also refer to: · Bryan Waller Procter (pseud. Barry Cornwall), English poet · Goodwin Procter, American law firm · Procter ' Gamble, consumer products multinational "
Marketing	marketing is a "social and managerial process by which individuals and groups obtain what they need and want through creating and exchanging products and values with others." It is an integrated process through which companies create value for customers and build strong customer relationships in order to capture value from customers in return.

marketing is used to create the customer, to keep the customer and to satisfy the customer. With the customer as the focus of its activities, it can be concluded that marketing management is one of the major components of business management.

Market environment

The market environment is a marketing term and refers to all of the forces outside of marketing that affect marketing management''s ability to build and maintain successful relationships with target customers. The market environment consists of both the macroenvironment and the microenvironment.

The microenvironment refers to the forces that are close to the company and affect its ability to serve its customers.

Product

When a product reaches the maturity stage of the product life cycle a company may choose to operate strategies to extend the life of the product. If the product is predicted to continue to be successful or an upgrade is soon to be released the company can use various methods to keep sales, else the product will be left as is to continue to the decline stage.

Examples of extension strategies are:

· Discounted price
· Increased advertising
· Accessing another market abroad

Another strategy is added value.

This is a widely used extension strategy.

Celebrity branding

Celebrity branding is a type of branding, in which a celebrity uses his or her status in society to promote a product, service or charity. Celebrity branding can take several different forms, from a celebrity simply appearing in advertisements for a product, service or charity, to a celebrity attending PR events, creating his or her own line of products or services, and/or using his or her name as a brand. The most popular forms of celebrity brand lines are for clothing and fragrances.

Competition

Co-operative competition is based upon promoting mutual survival - "everyone wins". Adam Smith''s "invisible hand" is a process where individuals compete to improve their level of happiness but compete in a cooperative manner through peaceful exchange and without violating other people. Cooperative competition focuses individuals/groups/organisms against the environment.

Ralph Lauren

Ralph Lauren is an American fashion designer and business executive. He is most notable for his Polo Ralph Lauren clothing brand.

Ralph Lauren was born Ralph Rueben Lifshitz in The Bronx to Ashkenazi Jewish immigrants from Belarus: Fraydl (Kotlar) and Frank Lifshitz, a house painter.

Taco Bell

Taco Bell is a restaurant chain based in Irvine, California, specializing in Mexican-inspired fast food. It is a subsidiary of Yum! Brands. Most restaurants are located in North America, but there are also many in other countries.

Wal-Mart

Wal-Mart Stores, Inc. is an American public corporation that runs a chain of large, discount department stores. It is the world''s largest public corporation by revenue, according to the 2008 Fortune Global 500.

Bean

Bean is a common name for large plant seeds of several genera of the family Fabaceae (alternately Leguminosae) used for human food or animal feed.

The whole young pods of Bean plants, if picked before the pods ripen and dry, can be tender enough to eat whole, whether cooked or raw. Thus the word "green Beans" means "green" in the sense of unripe (many are in fact, not green in color), as the Beans inside the pods of green Beans are too small to comprise a significant part of the cooked fruit.

Distribution

Distribution (or place) is one of the four elements of marketing mix. An organization or set of organizations (go-betweens) involved in the process of making a product or service available for use or consumption by a consumer or business user.

The other three parts of the marketing mix are product, pricing, and promotion.

Sale

A sale is the pinnacle activity involved in selling products or services in return for money or other compensation. It is an act of completion of a commercial activity.

A sale is completed by the seller, the owner of the goods.

Promotion

Promotion involves disseminating information about a product, product line, brand, or company. It is one of the four key aspects of the marketing mix. (The other three elements are product marketing, pricing, and distribution). P>Promotion is generally sub-divided into two parts:

· Above the line Promotion: Promotion in the media (e.g. TV, radio, newspapers, Internet and Mobile Phones) in which the advertiser pays an advertising agency to place the ad
· Below the line Promotion: All other Promotion. Much of this is intended to be subtle enough for the consumer to be unaware that Promotion is taking place. E.g. sponsorship, product placement, endorsements, sales Promotion, merchandising, direct mail, personal selling, public relations, trade shows

Television

television is a widely used telecommunication medium for transmitting and receiving moving images, either monochromatic ("black and white") or color, usually accompanied by sound. "television" may also refer specifically to a television set, television programming or television transmission.

Commercially available since the late 1930s, the television set has become a common communications receiver in homes, businesses and institutions, particularly as a source of entertainment and news.

Dangerous goods

dangerous goods,), are solids, liquids, other living organisms, property, or the environment. They are often subject to chemical regulations. dangerous goods include materials that are radioactive, flammable, explosive or corrosive, oxidizers or asphyxiants, biohazardous, toxic, pathogen or allergen substances and organisms.

Advertising Age

Advertising Age (or AdAge) is a magazine, delivering news, analysis and data on marketing and media. The magazine was started as a broadsheet newspaper in Chicago in 1930. Today, its content appears in a print weekly distributed around the world and on many electronic platforms, including: AdAge.com, daily e-mail newsletters called Ad Age Daily, Ad Age''s Mediaworks and Ad Age Digital; weekly newsletters such as Madison ' Vine (about branded entertainment) and Ad Age China; podcasts called Why It Matters and various videos. AdAge.com also features a bookstore and a number of blogs, some created by the publication''s editorial team, others, such as Small Agency Diary are created by members of the Ad Age community.

Branded entertainment	Branded entertainment, also known as branded content or advertainment, is an entertainment-based vehicle that is funded by and complementary to a brand"s marketing strategy. The purpose of a Branded entertainment program is to give a brand the opportunity to communicate its image to its target audience in an original way, by creating positive links between the brand and the program. Anything you do outside of work, money spent on activities outside "necessary" is entertainment.
Department Store	A Department store is a retail establishment which specializes in satisfying a wide range of the consumer"s personal and residential durable goods product needs; and at the same time offering the consumer a choice multiple merchandise lines, at variable price points, in all product categories. Department stores usually sell products including apparel, furniture, home appliances, electronics, and additionally select other lines of products such as paint, hardware, toiletries, cosmetics, photographic equipment, jewelery, toys, and sporting goods. Certain Department stores are further classified as discount Department stores.
Marketing Research	marketing research is the systematic gathering, recording, and analysis of data about issues relating to marketing products and services. The term is commonly interchanged with market research; however, expert practitioners may wish to draw a distinction, in that market research is concerned specifically with markets, while marketing research is concerned specifically about marketing processes. marketing research is often partitioned into two sets of categorical pairs, either by target market: · Consumer marketing research, and · Business-to-business marketing research Or, alternatively, by methodological approach: · Qualitative marketing research, and · Quantitative marketing research Consumer marketing research is a form of applied sociology that concentrates on understanding the preferences, attitudes, and behaviors of consumers in a market-based economy, and it aims to understand the effects and comparative success of marketing campaigns. The field of consumer marketing research as a statistical science was pioneered by Arthur Nielsen with the founding of the ACNielsen Company in 1923.
Sears	Sears, Roebuck and Co., commonly known as Sears, is an American mid-range chain of international department stores, founded by Richard Warren Sears and Alvah Roebuck in the late 19th century. From its mail order beginnings, the company grew to become the largest retailer in the United States by the mid-20th century, and its catalogs became famous. Competition and changes in the demographics of its customer base challenged the company after World War II as its rural and inner city strongholds shrank and the suburban markets grew.
Toy	A Toy is an object used in play. Toy s are usually associated with children and pets, but it is not unusual for adult humans and some non-domesticated animals to play with Toy s. Many items are manufactured to serve as Toy s, but goods, or (game-centric) services produced for other purposes can also be used as Toy s.
Category killer	Category killer is a term used in marketing and strategic management to describe a product, service, brand, whether real or virtual. Many existing firms will leave the industry, thereby increasing the industry"s concentration ratio.

Mass customization	Mass customization, in marketing, manufacturing, call centres and management, is the use of flexible computer-aided manufacturing systems to produce custom output. Those systems combine the low unit costs of mass production processes with the flexibility of individual customization. "Mass customization" is the new frontier in business competition for both manufacturing and service industries.
Advertising campaign	An Advertising campaign is a series of advertisement messages that share a single idea and theme which make up an integrated marketing communication (IMC). Advertising campaigns appear in different media across a specific time frame. The critical part of making an Advertising campaign is determining a champion theme as it sets the tone for the individual advertisements and other forms of marketing communications that will be used.
Direct marketing	Direct marketing is a sub-discipline and type of marketing. There are two main definitional characteristics which distinguish it from other types of marketing. The first is that it attempts to send its messages directly to consumers, without the use of intervening media.
Integrated marketing communications	integrated marketing communications is a term used to describe a holistic approach to marketing communication. It aims to ensure consistency of message and the complementary use of media. The concept includes online and offline marketing channels.
Marketing communication	marketing communications (or MarCom or Integrated marketing communications) are messages and related media used to communicate with a market. Those who practice advertising, branding, direct marketing, graphic design, marketing, packaging, promotion, publicity, sponsorship, public relations, sales, sales promotion and online marketing are termed marketing communicators, marketing communication managers, or more briefly as marcom managers. Traditionally, marketing communication practitioners focus on the creation and execution of printed marketing collateral; however, academic and professional research developed the practice to use strategic elements of branding and marketing in order to ensure consistency of message delivery throughout an organization - the same "look ' feel".
Sales promotion	Sales promotion is one of the four aspects of promotional mix. (The other three parts of the promotional mix are advertising, personal selling, and publicity/public relations.) Media and non-media marketing communication are employed for a pre-determined, limited time to increase consumer demand, stimulate market demand or improve product availability.
Twinkie	A Twinkie is a "Golden Sponge Cake with Creamy Filling" popular in the United States and elsewhere in North America. Introduced by natives, it is distributed by Hostess, which is owned by Dallas-based Interstate Bakeries Corporation. Twinkies are the brainchild of James A. Dewar, one of Continental"s bakers. Realizing that several machines used to make cream-filled strawberry shortcake sat idle when strawberries were out of season, Dewar conceived a snack cake filled with banana cream, which would be dubbed the Twinkie.

Copy platform

Plan for use by the copywriter that defines the basic theme of the advertising campaign and serves as a guide for writing an advertisement; , the Copy platform discusses the issues to be considered and describes the fundamental elements, such as slogans, visual symbols, and associations, to be built around the product (or service). It will also discuss the profile of the target audience, the product or service"s claims, the kinds of appeals to be used, the customer needs that the product or service will satisfy, and the image to be created, as well as the style, tone, and implications of the finished advertisement.

Marketing

marketing is a "social and managerial process by which individuals and groups obtain what they need and want through creating and exchanging products and values with others." It is an integrated process through which companies create value for customers and build strong customer relationships in order to capture value from customers in return. marketing is used to create the customer, to keep the customer and to satisfy the customer. With the customer as the focus of its activities, it can be concluded that marketing management is one of the major components of business management.

Phenomenon

A phenomenon is any observable occurrence. In popular usage, a phenomenon often refers to an extraordinary event. In scientific usage, a phenomenon is any event that is observable, however commonplace it might be, even if it requires the use of instrumentation to observe it.

Situation analysis

Situation analysis is a marketing term, and involves evaluating the situation and trends in a particular company"s market. Situation analysis is often called the "three c"s", which refers to the three major elements that must be studied:

· Customers
· Costs
· Competition

The number of "c"s" is sometimes extended to four, five, or even six, with "Collaboration", "Company", and "Competitive advantage".

· Marketing mix
· SWOT analysis .

SWOT analysis

SWOT analysis is a strategic planning method used to evaluate the Strengths, Weaknesses, Opportunities, and Threats involved in a project or in a business venture. It involves specifying the objective of the business venture or project and identifying the internal and external factors that are favorable and unfavorable to achieving that objective. The technique is credited to Albert Humphrey, who led a research project at Stanford University in the 1960s and 1970s using data from Fortune 500 companies.

Audit

The general definition of an Audit is an evaluation of a person, organization, system, process, enterprise, project or product. Audits are performed to ascertain the validity and reliability of information; also to provide an assessment of a system"s internal control. The goal of an Audit is to express an opinion on the person / organization/system (etc) in question, under evaluation based on work done on a test basis.

Sale

A sale is the pinnacle activity involved in selling products or services in return for money or other compensation. It is an act of completion of a commercial activity.

A sale is completed by the seller, the owner of the goods.

Toy

A Toy is an object used in play. Toy s are usually associated with children and pets, but it is not unusual for adult humans and some non-domesticated animals to play with Toy s. Many items are manufactured to serve as Toy s, but goods, or (game-centric) services produced for other purposes can also be used as Toy s.

Internality

An internality is a term used in behavioral economics to describe those types of behaviors that impose costs on a person in the long-run that are not taken into account when making decisions in the present. Classical Economics discourages government from creating legislation that targets internalities, because it is assumed that the consumer takes these personal costs into account when paying for the good that causes the internality. For example, cigarettes should be taxed because of the negative consumption externalities that they impose, such as second-hand smoke, not because the smoker harms him or herself by smoking.

Trend analysis

The term "Trend analysis" refers to the concept of collecting information and attempting to spot a pattern, in the information. In some fields of study, the term "Trend analysis" has more formally-defined meanings.

In project management Trend analysis is a mathematical technique that uses historical results to predict future outcome.

External

In economics, an externality or spillover of an economic transaction is an impact on a party that is not directly involved in the transaction. In such a case, prices do not reflect the full costs or benefits in production or consumption of a product or service. An advantageous impact is called an external benefit or positive externality, while a detrimental impact is called an external cost or negative externality.

Standard

A technical standard is an established norm or requirement. It is usually a formal document that establishes uniform engineering or technical criteria, methods, processes and practices.

A technical standard can also be a controlled artifact or similar formal means used for calibration.

Leo Burnett

Leo Burnett (October 21, 1891 - June 7, 1971) was an advertising executive famous for creating such icons as the Jolly Green Giant, the Marlboro Man, Toucan Sam, Charlie the Tuna, Morris the Cat, the Pillsbury Doughboy, the 7up "Spot", and Tony the Tiger.

Burnett was named by Time magazine as one of the 100 most influential people of the 20th century.

Born in St. Johns, Michigan, he studied journalism at the University of Michigan.

Consumer

Consumer is a broad label for any individuals or households that use goods and services generated within the economy. The concept of a Consumer is used in different contexts, so that the usage and significance of the term may vary.

Typically when business people and economists talk of Consumers they are talking about person as Consumer, an aggregated commodity item with little individuality other than that expressed in the buy/not-buy decision.

Procter ' Gamble

Procter is a surname, and may also refer to:

· Bryan Waller Procter (pseud. Barry Cornwall), English poet
· Goodwin Procter, American law firm
· Procter ' Gamble, consumer products multinational "

Research

research is defined as human activity based on intellectual application in the investigation of matter. The primary purpose for applied research is discovering, interpreting, and the development of methods and systems for the advancement of human knowledge on a wide variety of scientific matters of our world and the universe. research can use the scientific method, but need not do so.

Product

When a product reaches the maturity stage of the product life cycle a company may choose to operate strategies to extend the life of the product. If the product is predicted to continue to be successful or an upgrade is soon to be released the company can use various methods to keep sales, else the product will be left as is to continue to the decline stage.

Examples of extension strategies are:

· Discounted price
· Increased advertising
· Accessing another market abroad

Another strategy is added value.

This is a widely used extension strategy.

Marketing Research

marketing research is the systematic gathering, recording, and analysis of data about issues relating to marketing products and services. The term is commonly interchanged with market research; however, expert practitioners may wish to draw a distinction, in that market research is concerned specifically with markets, while marketing research is concerned specifically about marketing processes.

marketing research is often partitioned into two sets of categorical pairs, either by target market:

· Consumer marketing research, and
· Business-to-business marketing research

Or, alternatively, by methodological approach:

· Qualitative marketing research, and
· Quantitative marketing research

Consumer marketing research is a form of applied sociology that concentrates on understanding the preferences, attitudes, and behaviors of consumers in a market-based economy, and it aims to understand the effects and comparative success of marketing campaigns. The field of consumer marketing research as a statistical science was pioneered by Arthur Nielsen with the founding of the ACNielsen Company in 1923.

Taco Bell

Taco Bell is a restaurant chain based in Irvine, California, specializing in Mexican-inspired fast food. It is a subsidiary of Yum! Brands. Most restaurants are located in North America, but there are also many in other countries.

VALS

The acronym VALS, is a psychographic segmentation. It was developed in the 1970s to explain changing U.S. values and lifestyles. It has since been reworked to enhance its ability to predict consumer behavior.

	According to the VALS Framework, groups of people are arranged in a rectangle and are based on two dimensions. The vertical dimension segments people based on the degree to which they are innovative and have resources such as income, education, self-confidence, intelligence, leadership skills, and energy.
Demographic	Demographics data are selected population characteristics as used in government, marketing or opinion research). Commonly-used Demographics include sex, race, age, income, disabilities, mobility (in terms of travel time to work or number of vehicles available), educational attainment, home ownership, employment status, and even location.
Psychographic	In the field of marketing, demographics, opinion research, and social research in general, psychographic variables are any attributes relating to personality, values, attitudes, interests, or lifestyles. They are also called IAO variables . They can be contrasted with demographic variables (such as age and gender), behavioral variables (such as usage rate or loyalty), and bizographic variables (such as industry, seniority and functional area.)
Celebrity branding	Celebrity branding is a type of branding, in which a celebrity uses his or her status in society to promote a product, service or charity. Celebrity branding can take several different forms, from a celebrity simply appearing in advertisements for a product, service or charity, to a celebrity attending PR events, creating his or her own line of products or services, and/or using his or her name as a brand. The most popular forms of celebrity brand lines are for clothing and fragrances.
Bean	Bean is a common name for large plant seeds of several genera of the family Fabaceae (alternately Leguminosae) used for human food or animal feed. The whole young pods of Bean plants, if picked before the pods ripen and dry, can be tender enough to eat whole, whether cooked or raw. Thus the word "green Beans" means "green" in the sense of unripe (many are in fact, not green in color), as the Beans inside the pods of green Beans are too small to comprise a significant part of the cooked fruit.
Competition	Co-operative competition is based upon promoting mutual survival - "everyone wins". Adam Smith"s "invisible hand" is a process where individuals compete to improve their level of happiness but compete in a cooperative manner through peaceful exchange and without violating other people. Cooperative competition focuses individuals/groups/organisms against the environment.
Resources	Human beings are also considered to be Resources because they have the ability to change raw materials into valuable Resources. The term Human Resources can also be defined as the skills, energies, talents, abilities and knowledge that are used for the production of goods or the rendering of services. While taking into account human beings as Resources, the following things have to be kept in mind: · The size of the population · The capabilities of the individuals in that population Many Resources cannot be consumed in their original form. They have to be processed in order to change them into more usable commodities.
Advertising campaign	An Advertising campaign is a series of advertisement messages that share a single idea and theme which make up an integrated marketing communication (IMC). Advertising campaigns appear in different media across a specific time frame.

The critical part of making an Advertising campaign is determining a champion theme as it sets the tone for the individual advertisements and other forms of marketing communications that will be used.

Competitive

competitiveness is a comparative concept of the ability and performance of a firm, sub-sector or country to sell and supply goods and/or services in a given market. Although widely used in economics and business management, the usefulness of the concept, particularly in the context of national competitiveness, is vigorously disputed by economists, such as Paul Krugman .

The term may also be applied to markets, where it is used to refer to the extent to which the market structure may be regarded as perfectly competitive.

Market analysis

A market analysis is a documented investigation of a Market that is used to inform a firm''s planning activities particularly around decision of: inventory, purchase, work force expansion/contraction, facility expansion, purchases of capital equipment, promotional activities, and many other aspects of a company.

Not all managers are asked to conduct a market analysis, but all managers must make decisions using market analysis data and understand how the data was derived. So all managers need a reasonable understanding of the tools most used for making sales forecasts and analyzing markets.

Department Store

A Department store is a retail establishment which specializes in satisfying a wide range of the consumer''s personal and residential durable goods product needs; and at the same time offering the consumer a choice multiple merchandise lines, at variable price points, in all product categories. Department stores usually sell products including apparel, furniture, home appliances, electronics, and additionally select other lines of products such as paint, hardware, toiletries, cosmetics, photographic equipment, jewelery, toys, and sporting goods. Certain Department stores are further classified as discount Department stores.

Consumer Confidence Index

The U.S. Consumer Confidence Index is an indicator designed to measure consumer confidence, which is defined as the degree of optimism on the state of the economy that consumers are expressing through their activities of savings and spending. Global consumer confidence is not measured. Country by country analysis indicates huge variance around the globe.

Qualitative research

Qualitative research is a field of inquiry applicable to many disciplines and subject matters. Qualitative research ers aim to gather an in-depth understanding of human behavior and the reasons that govern such behavior. The qualitative method investigates the why and how of decision making, not just what, where, when.

Want

In economics, a Want is something that is desired. It is said that people have unlimited Want s, but limited resources. Each person has Want s.

Account planning

"account planning is the discipline that brings the consumer into the process of developing advertising. To be truly effective, advertising must be both distinctive and relevant, and planning helps on both counts." - Chris Cowpe

account planning is a job title that exists in most London and UK advertising agencies. account planning gained a foothold in the U.S. in the mid 80''s and has been growing ever since.

Focus group

A Focus group is a form of qualitative research in which a group of people are asked about their attitude towards a product, service, concept, advertisement, idea, or packaging. Questions are asked in an interactive group setting where participants are free to talk with other group members.

The first Focus groups were created at the Bureau of Applied Social Research by associate director, sociologist Robert K. Merton.

Projective test

A Projective test in psychology, is a personality test designed to let a person respond to ambiguous stimuli, presumably revealing hidden emotions and internal conflicts. This is different from an "objective test" in which responses are analyzed according to a universal standard (for example, a multiple choice exam.) The responses to Projective test s are content analyzed for meaning rather than being based on presuppositions about meaning, as is the case with objective tests.

Theory

Although the scientific meaning is by far the more commonly used in academic discourse, it is hardly the only one used, and it would be a mistake to assume from the outset that a given use of the term "theory" in academic literature or discourse is a reference to a scientific or empirically-based theory.

Even so, since the use of the term theory in scientific or empirical inquiry is the more common one, it will be discussed first. (Other usages follow in the section labeled "Theories formally and generally.")

A theory, in the scientific sense of the word, is an analytic structure designed to explain a set of empirical observations. A scientific theory does two things:

· it identifies this set of distinct observations as a class of phenomena, and

· makes assertions about the underlying reality that brings about or affects this class.

In the scientific or empirical tradition, the term "theory" is reserved for ideas which meet baseline requirements about the kinds of empirical observations made, the methods of classification used, and the consistency of the theory in its application among members of the class to which it pertains.

Laddering

Laddering is an investment technique that requires investors to purchase multiple financial products with different maturity dates.

Laddering avoids the risk of reinvesting a big portion of assets in an unfavorable financial environment. For example, a person has both a 2015 matured CD and a 2018 matured CD. Even if the interest rate drops fairly low in 2015 when one certificate is to be renewed, half of the income is locked in until 2018.

Point

In typography, a point is the smallest unit of measure, being a subdivision of the larger pica. It is commonly abbreviated as pt. The traditional printer''s point, from the era of hot metal typesetting and presswork, varied between 0.18 and 0.4 mm depending on various definitions of the foot.

Today, the traditional point has been supplanted by the desktop publishing point (also called the PostScript point), which has been rounded to an even 72 points to the inch (1 point = $^{127}/_{360}$ mm ≈ 0.353 mm).

Value

A personal and cultural value is a relative ethic value, an assumption upon which implementation can be extrapolated. A value system is a set of consistent values and measures that is soo not true. A principle value is a foundation upon which other values and measures of integrity are based.

FUBU	FUBU is a clothing company. It includes casual wear, sports wear, a suit collection, eyewear, belts, and shoes. The name is a backronym for "FUBU", indicating that the product line was produced by black Americans for a primarily black American market.
Psychosocial	The term psychosocial refers to one in psychological development in and interaction with a social environment. The individual is not necessarily fully aware of this relationship with his or her environment. It was first commonly used by psychologist Erik Erikson in his stages of social development.
Media Market	A Media market, broadcast market, media region, designated market area (DMA), Television Market Area (FCC term) or simply market is a region where the population can receive the same (or similar) television and radio station offerings, and may also include other types of media including newspapers and Internet content. They can coincide with metropolitan areas, though rural regions with few significant population centers can also be designated as markets. Conversely, very large metropolitan areas can sometimes be subdivided into multiple segments.
Survey research	Survey research a research method involving the use of questionnaires and/or statistical surveys to gather data about people and their thoughts and behaviours.
Telephone	The telephone is a telecommunications device that transmits and receives sound, most commonly the human voice. It is one of the most common household appliances in the developed world, and has long been considered indispensable to business, industry and government. The word telephone has been adapted to many languages and is widely recognized around the world.
Questionnaire	A questionnaire is a research instrument consisting of a series of questions and other prompts for the purpose of gathering information from respondents. Although they are often designed for statistical analysis of the responses, this is not always the case. The questionnaire was invented by Sir Francis Galton.

Procter ' Gamble	Procter is a surname, and may also refer to: · Bryan Waller Procter (pseud. Barry Cornwall), English poet · Goodwin Procter, American law firm · Procter ' Gamble, consumer products multinational ''
Market analysis	A market analysis is a documented investigation of a Market that is used to inform a firm''s planning activities particularly around decision of: inventory, purchase, work force expansion/contraction, facility expansion, purchases of capital equipment, promotional activities, and many other aspects of a company. Not all managers are asked to conduct a market analysis, but all managers must make decisions using market analysis data and understand how the data was derived. So all managers need a reasonable understanding of the tools most used for making sales forecasts and analyzing markets.
Product	When a product reaches the maturity stage of the product life cycle a company may choose to operate strategies to extend the life of the product. If the product is predicted to continue to be successful or an upgrade is soon to be released the company can use various methods to keep sales, else the product will be left as is to continue to the decline stage. Examples of extension strategies are: · Discounted price · Increased advertising · Accessing another market abroad Another strategy is added value. This is a widely used extension strategy.
Marketing	marketing is a "social and managerial process by which individuals and groups obtain what they need and want through creating and exchanging products and values with others." It is an integrated process through which companies create value for customers and build strong customer relationships in order to capture value from customers in return. marketing is used to create the customer, to keep the customer and to satisfy the customer. With the customer as the focus of its activities, it can be concluded that marketing management is one of the major components of business management.
Marketing Management	Marketing management is a business discipline which is focused on the practical application of marketing techniques and the management of a firm''s marketing resources and activities. Marketing managers are often responsible for influencing the level, timing, and composition of customer demand accepted definition of the term. In part, this is because the role of a marketing manager can vary significantly based on a business'' size, corporate culture, and industry context.
Research	research is defined as human activity based on intellectual application in the investigation of matter. The primary purpose for applied research is discovering, interpreting, and the development of methods and systems for the advancement of human knowledge on a wide variety of scientific matters of our world and the universe. research can use the scientific method, but need not do so.

Sale	A sale is the pinnacle activity involved in selling products or services in return for money or other compensation. It is an act of completion of a commercial activity. A sale is completed by the seller, the owner of the goods.
Index number	An Index number is an economic data figure reflecting price or quantity compared with a standard or base value. The base usually equals 100 and the Index number is usually expressed as 100 times the ratio to the base value. For example, if a commodity costs twice as much in 1970 as it did in 1960, its Index number would be 200 relative to 1960. Index numbers are used especially to compare business activity, the cost of living, and employment.
Media Market	A Media market, broadcast market, media region, designated market area (DMA), Television Market Area (FCC term) or simply market is a region where the population can receive the same (or similar) television and radio station offerings, and may also include other types of media including newspapers and Internet content. They can coincide with metropolitan areas, though rural regions with few significant population centers can also be designated as markets. Conversely, very large metropolitan areas can sometimes be subdivided into multiple segments.
Demographic	Demographics data are selected population characteristics as used in government, marketing or opinion research). Commonly-used Demographics include sex, race, age, income, disabilities, mobility (in terms of travel time to work or number of vehicles available), educational attainment, home ownership, employment status, and even location.
Dangerous goods	dangerous goods,), are solids, liquids, other living organisms, property, or the environment. They are often subject to chemical regulations. dangerous goods include materials that are radioactive, flammable, explosive or corrosive, oxidizers or asphyxiants, biohazardous, toxic, pathogen or allergen substances and organisms.
Projective test	A Projective test in psychology, is a personality test designed to let a person respond to ambiguous stimuli, presumably revealing hidden emotions and internal conflicts. This is different from an "objective test" in which responses are analyzed according to a universal standard (for example, a multiple choice exam.) The responses to Projective test s are content analyzed for meaning rather than being based on presuppositions about meaning, as is the case with objective tests.
Semantic differential	Semantic differential is a type of a rating scale designed to measure the connotative meaning of objects, events, and concepts. The connotations are used to derive the attitude towards the given object, event or concept. Osgood"s Semantic differential was designed to measure the connotative meaning of concepts.
Likert scale	A Likert scale is a psychometric scale commonly used in questionnaires, and is the most widely used scale in survey research. When responding to a Likert questionnaire item, respondents specify their level of agreement to a statement. The scale is named after its inventor, psychologist Rensis Likert.
Accounting profit	Accounting profit is the difference between price and the costs of bringing to market whatever it is that is accounted as an enterprise (whether by harvest, extraction, manufacture) in terms of the component costs of delivered goods and/or services and any operating or other expenses. A key difficulty in measuring profit is in defining costs. Pure economic monetary profits can be zero or negative even in competitive equilibrium when accounted monetized costs exceed monetized price.
Word association	Word Association is a common word game involving an exchange of words that are associated together.

Once an original word has been chosen, usually randomly or arbitrarily, a player will find a word that they associate with it and make it known to all the players, usually by saying it aloud or writing it down as the next item on a list of words so far used. The next player must then do the same with this previous word.

Celebrity branding

Celebrity branding is a type of branding, in which a celebrity uses his or her status in society to promote a product, service or charity. Celebrity branding can take several different forms, from a celebrity simply appearing in advertisements for a product, service or charity, to a celebrity attending PR events, creating his or her own line of products or services, and/or using his or her name as a brand. The most popular forms of celebrity brand lines are for clothing and fragrances.

Competition

Co-operative competition is based upon promoting mutual survival - "everyone wins". Adam Smith"s "invisible hand" is a process where individuals compete to improve their level of happiness but compete in a cooperative manner through peaceful exchange and without violating other people. Cooperative competition focuses individuals/groups/organisms against the environment.

Role

A role or a social role is a set of connected behaviors, rights and obligations as conceptualized by actors in a social situation. It is an expected behavior in a given individual social status and social position. It is vital to both functionalist and interactionist understandings of society.

Storytelling

Storytelling is the conveying of events in words, images, and sounds often by improvisation or embellishment. Stories or narratives have been shared in every culture and in every land as a means of entertainment, education, preservation of culture and in order to instill moral values. Crucial elements of stories and Storytelling include plot and characters, as well as the narrative point of view.

Test-retest

test-retest is a statistical method used to examine how reliable a test is: A test is performed twice, e.g., the same test is given to a group of subjects at two different times. Each subject should score different than the other subjects, but if the test is reliable then each subject should score the same in both test.

Valentin Rousson, Theo Gasser, and Burkhardt Seifert, (2002) "Assessing intrarater, interrater and test-retest reliability of continuous measurements," Statistics in Medicine 21:3431-3446.

Competitive

competitiveness is a comparative concept of the ability and performance of a firm, sub-sector or country to sell and supply goods and/or services in a given market. Although widely used in economics and business management, the usefulness of the concept, particularly in the context of national competitiveness, is vigorously disputed by economists, such as Paul Krugman .

The term may also be applied to markets, where it is used to refer to the extent to which the market structure may be regarded as perfectly competitive.

Walt Disney

Walter Elias "Walt" Disney (December 5, 1901 - December 15, 1966) was an American film producer, director, screenwriter, voice actor, animator, entrepreneur, entertainer, international icon and philanthropist. Disney is famous for his influence in the field of entertainment during the twentieth century. As the co-founder (with his brother Roy O. Disney) of Walt Disney Productions, Disney became one of the best-known motion picture producers in the world.

Report

In writing, a report is a document characterized by information or other content reflective of inquiry or investigation, which is tailored to the context of a given situation and audience. The purpose of report s is usually to inform. However, report s may include persuasive elements, such as recommendations, suggestions, or other motivating conclusions that indicate possible future actions the report reader might take.

Distribution

Distribution (or place) is one of the four elements of marketing mix. An organization or set of organizations (go-betweens) involved in the process of making a product or service available for use or consumption by a consumer or business user.

The other three parts of the marketing mix are product, pricing, and promotion.

Marketing mix

The four main fields of the marketing mix.

The marketing mix is generally accepted as the use and specification of the "four Ps" describing the strategy position of a product in the marketplace. The "marketing mix" is a set of controllable, tactical marketing tools that work together to achieve company"s objectives. One version of the marketing mix originated in 1948 when James Culliton said that a marketing decision should be a result of something similar to a recipe.

Perceptual mapping

Perceptual mapping is a graphics technique used by asset marketers that attempts to visually display the perceptions of customers or potential customers. Typically the position of a product, product line, brand, or company is displayed relative to their competition.

Perceptual maps can have any number of dimensions but the most common is two dimensions.

Mind control

Mind control (also referred to as brainwashing, coercive persuasion, and thought reform) refers to a broad range of psychological tactics thought to subvert an individual"s control of his or her own thinking, behavior, emotions).

Reporting

With the dramatic expansion of information technology, and the desire for increased competitiveness in corporations, there has been an increase in the use of computing power to produce unified reports which join different views of the enterprise in one place. Termed Enterprise reporting, this process involves querying data sources with different logical models to produce a human readable report. A computer user has to query the Human Resources databases and the Capital Improvements databases to show how efficiently space is being used across an entire corporation.

Promotion

Promotion involves disseminating information about a product, product line, brand, or company. It is one of the four key aspects of the marketing mix. (The other three elements are product marketing, pricing, and distribution). P>Promotion is generally sub-divided into two parts:

· Above the line Promotion: Promotion in the media (e.g. TV, radio, newspapers, Internet and Mobile Phones) in which the advertiser pays an advertising agency to place the ad
· Below the line Promotion: All other Promotion. Much of this is intended to be subtle enough for the consumer to be unaware that Promotion is taking place. E.g. sponsorship, product placement, endorsements, sales Promotion, merchandising, direct mail, personal selling, public relations, trade shows

Sales promotion	Sales promotion is one of the four aspects of promotional mix. (The other three parts of the promotional mix are advertising, personal selling, and publicity/public relations.) Media and non-media marketing communication are employed for a pre-determined, limited time to increase consumer demand, stimulate market demand or improve product availability.

Celebrity branding	Celebrity branding is a type of branding, in which a celebrity uses his or her status in society to promote a product, service or charity. Celebrity branding can take several different forms, from a celebrity simply appearing in advertisements for a product, service or charity, to a celebrity attending PR events, creating his or her own line of products or services, and/or using his or her name as a brand. The most popular forms of celebrity brand lines are for clothing and fragrances.
Advertising Age	Advertising Age (or AdAge) is a magazine, delivering news, analysis and data on marketing and media. The magazine was started as a broadsheet newspaper in Chicago in 1930. Today, its content appears in a print weekly distributed around the world and on many electronic platforms, including: AdAge.com, daily e-mail newsletters called Ad Age Daily, Ad Age"s Mediaworks and Ad Age Digital; weekly newsletters such as Madison ' Vine (about branded entertainment) and Ad Age China; podcasts called Why It Matters and various videos. AdAge.com also features a bookstore and a number of blogs, some created by the publication"s editorial team, others, such as Small Agency Diary are created by members of the Ad Age community.
Competition	Co-operative competition is based upon promoting mutual survival - "everyone wins". Adam Smith"s "invisible hand" is a process where individuals compete to improve their level of happiness but compete in a cooperative manner through peaceful exchange and without violating other people. Cooperative competition focuses individuals/groups/organisms against the environment.
Brand equity	Brand equity refers to the marketing effects or outcomes that accrue to a product with its brand name compared with those that would accrue if the same product did not have the brand name . And, at the root of these marketing effects is consumers" knowledge. In other words, consumers" knowledge about a brand makes manufacturers/advertisers respond differently or adopt appropriately adept measures for the marketing of the brand .
Flowchart	A flowchart is a common type of diagram, that represents an algorithm or process, showing the steps as boxes of various kinds, and their order by connecting these with arrows. flowcharts are used in analyzing, designing, documenting or managing a process or program in various fields. The first structured method for documenting process flow, the "flow process chart", was introduced by Frank Gilbreth to members of ASME in 1921 as the presentation "Process Charts--First Steps in Finding the One Best Way".
Procter ' Gamble	Procter is a surname, and may also refer to: · Bryan Waller Procter (pseud. Barry Cornwall), English poet · Goodwin Procter, American law firm · Procter ' Gamble, consumer products multinational "
Wal-Mart	Wal-Mart Stores, Inc. is an American public corporation that runs a chain of large, discount department stores. It is the world"s largest public corporation by revenue, according to the 2008 Fortune Global 500.
Quality	Quality in business, engineering and manufacturing has a pragmatic interpretation as the non-inferiority or superiority of something. Quality is a perceptual, conditional and somewhat subjective attribute and may be understood differently by different people. Consumers may focus on the specification Quality of a product/service, or how it compares to competitors in the marketplace.

Hammer

A hammer is a tool meant to deliver an impact to an object. The most common uses are for driving nails, fitting parts, forging metal and breaking up objects. hammers are often designed for a specific purpose, and vary widely in their shape and structure.

Promotion

Promotion involves disseminating information about a product, product line, brand, or company. It is one of the four key aspects of the marketing mix. (The other three elements are product marketing, pricing, and distribution). P>Promotion is generally sub-divided into two parts:

· Above the line Promotion: Promotion in the media (e.g. TV, radio, newspapers, Internet and Mobile Phones) in which the advertiser pays an advertising agency to place the ad
· Below the line Promotion: All other Promotion. Much of this is intended to be subtle enough for the consumer to be unaware that Promotion is taking place. E.g. sponsorship, product placement, endorsements, sales Promotion, merchandising, direct mail, personal selling, public relations, trade shows

Taco Bell

Taco Bell is a restaurant chain based in Irvine, California, specializing in Mexican-inspired fast food. It is a subsidiary of Yum! Brands. Most restaurants are located in North America, but there are also many in other countries.

Twinkie

A Twinkie is a "Golden Sponge Cake with Creamy Filling" popular in the United States and elsewhere in North America. Introduced by natives, it is distributed by Hostess, which is owned by Dallas-based Interstate Bakeries Corporation.

Twinkies are the brainchild of James A. Dewar, one of Continental"s bakers. Realizing that several machines used to make cream-filled strawberry shortcake sat idle when strawberries were out of season, Dewar conceived a snack cake filled with banana cream, which would be dubbed the Twinkie.

Competitive

competitiveness is a comparative concept of the ability and performance of a firm, sub-sector or country to sell and supply goods and/or services in a given market. Although widely used in economics and business management, the usefulness of the concept, particularly in the context of national competitiveness, is vigorously disputed by economists, such as Paul Krugman .

The term may also be applied to markets, where it is used to refer to the extent to which the market structure may be regarded as perfectly competitive.

Marketing

marketing is a "social and managerial process by which individuals and groups obtain what they need and want through creating and exchanging products and values with others." It is an integrated process through which companies create value for customers and build strong customer relationships in order to capture value from customers in return. marketing is used to create the customer, to keep the customer and to satisfy the customer. With the customer as the focus of its activities, it can be concluded that marketing management is one of the major components of business management.

Marketing Research

marketing research is the systematic gathering, recording, and analysis of data about issues relating to marketing products and services. The term is commonly interchanged with market research; however, expert practitioners may wish to draw a distinction, in that market research is concerned specifically with markets, while marketing research is concerned specifically about marketing processes.

marketing research is often partitioned into two sets of categorical pairs, either by target market:

· Consumer marketing research, and
· Business-to-business marketing research

Or, alternatively, by methodological approach:

· Qualitative marketing research, and
· Quantitative marketing research

Consumer marketing research is a form of applied sociology that concentrates on understanding the preferences, attitudes, and behaviors of consumers in a market-based economy, and it aims to understand the effects and comparative success of marketing campaigns. The field of consumer marketing research as a statistical science was pioneered by Arthur Nielsen with the founding of the ACNielsen Company in 1923.

Report

In writing, a report is a document characterized by information or other content reflective of inquiry or investigation, which is tailored to the context of a given situation and audience. The purpose of report s is usually to inform. However, report s may include persuasive elements, such as recommendations, suggestions, or other motivating conclusions that indicate possible future actions the report reader might take.

Goal

A Goal or objective is a projected state of affairs that a person or a system plans or intends to achieve--a personal or organizational desired end-point in some sort of assumed development. Many people endeavor to reach Goals within a finite time by setting deadlines.

A desire or an intention becomes a Goal if and only if one activates an action for achieving it .

Technology

Technology is a broad concept that deals with an animal species" usage and knowledge of tools and crafts, and how it affects an animal species" ability to control and adapt to its environment. Technology is a term with origins in the Greek "technologia", "τεχνολογÎÂ¯α" -- "techne", "τÎÂχνη" and "logia", "λογÎÂ¯α" ("saying".) However, a strict definition is elusive; "Technology" can refer to material objects of use to humanity, such as machines, hardware or utensils, but can also encompass broader themes, including systems, methods of organization, and techniques.

Purpose

purpose is the cognitive awareness in cause and effect linking for achieving a goal in a given system, whether human or machine. Its most general sense is the anticipated result which guides decision making in choosing appropriate actions within a range of strategies in the process (a conceptual scheme) based on varying degrees of ambiguity about the knowledge that creates the contextualisation for the action. purpose serves to change the state of conditions in a given environment, usually to one with a perceived better set of conditions or parameters from the previous state.

Theory

Although the scientific meaning is by far the more commonly used in academic discourse, it is hardly the only one used, and it would be a mistake to assume from the outset that a given use of the term "theory" in academic literature or discourse is a reference to a scientific or empirically-based theory.

Even so, since the use of the term theory in scientific or empirical inquiry is the more common one, it will be discussed first. (Other usages follow in the section labeled "Theories formally and generally.")

A theory, in the scientific sense of the word, is an analytic structure designed to explain a set of empirical observations. A scientific theory does two things:

· it identifies this set of distinct observations as a class of phenomena, and

· makes assertions about the underlying reality that brings about or affects this class.

In the scientific or empirical tradition, the term "theory" is reserved for ideas which meet baseline requirements about the kinds of empirical observations made, the methods of classification used, and the consistency of the theory in its application among members of the class to which it pertains.

Yield

Yield is the compound rate of return that includes the effect of reinvesting interest or dividends.

To the right is an example of a stock investment of one share purchased at the beginning of the year for $100.

· The quarterly dividend is reinvested at the quarter-end stock price.
· The number of shares purchased each quarter = ($ Dividend)/($ Stock Price).
· The final investment value of $103.02 is a 3.02% Yield on the initial investment of $100. This is the compound Yield, and this return can be considered to be the return on the investment of $100.

To calculate the rate of return, the investor includes the reinvested dividends in the total investment. The investor received a total of $4.06 in dividends over the year, all of which were reinvested, so the investment amount increased by $4.06.

· Total Investment = Cost Basis = $100 + $4.06 = $104.06.
· Capital gain/loss = $103.02 - $104.06 = -$1.04 (a capital loss)
· ($4.06 dividends - $1.04 capital loss) / $104.06 total investment = 2.9% ROI

The disadvantage of this ROI calculation is that it does not take into account the fact that not all the money was invested during the entire year (the dividend reinvestments occurred throughout the year).

Celebrity branding	Celebrity branding is a type of branding, in which a celebrity uses his or her status in society to promote a product, service or charity. Celebrity branding can take several different forms, from a celebrity simply appearing in advertisements for a product, service or charity, to a celebrity attending PR events, creating his or her own line of products or services, and/or using his or her name as a brand. The most popular forms of celebrity brand lines are for clothing and fragrances.
Advertising Age	Advertising Age (or AdAge) is a magazine, delivering news, analysis and data on marketing and media. The magazine was started as a broadsheet newspaper in Chicago in 1930. Today, its content appears in a print weekly distributed around the world and on many electronic platforms, including: AdAge.com, daily e-mail newsletters called Ad Age Daily, Ad Age''s Mediaworks and Ad Age Digital; weekly newsletters such as Madison ' Vine (about branded entertainment) and Ad Age China; podcasts called Why It Matters and various videos. AdAge.com also features a bookstore and a number of blogs, some created by the publication''s editorial team, others, such as Small Agency Diary are created by members of the Ad Age community.
Consideration	Consideration is the legal concept of value in connection with contracts. It is anything of value in the common sense, promised to another when making a contract. It can take the form of money, physical objects, services, promised actions, or even abstinence from a future action.
Procter ' Gamble	Procter is a surname, and may also refer to: · Bryan Waller Procter (pseud. Barry Cornwall), English poet · Goodwin Procter, American law firm · Procter ' Gamble, consumer products multinational ''
Dangerous goods	dangerous goods,), are solids, liquids, other living organisms, property, or the environment. They are often subject to chemical regulations. dangerous goods include materials that are radioactive, flammable, explosive or corrosive, oxidizers or asphyxiants, biohazardous, toxic, pathogen or allergen substances and organisms.
Brand equity	Brand equity refers to the marketing effects or outcomes that accrue to a product with its brand name compared with those that would accrue if the same product did not have the brand name . And, at the root of these marketing effects is consumers'' knowledge. In other words, consumers'' knowledge about a brand makes manufacturers/advertisers respond differently or adopt appropriately adept measures for the marketing of the brand .
Marketing	marketing is a "social and managerial process by which individuals and groups obtain what they need and want through creating and exchanging products and values with others." It is an integrated process through which companies create value for customers and build strong customer relationships in order to capture value from customers in return. marketing is used to create the customer, to keep the customer and to satisfy the customer. With the customer as the focus of its activities, it can be concluded that marketing management is one of the major components of business management.
Marketing communication	marketing communications (or MarCom or Integrated marketing communications) are messages and related media used to communicate with a market. Those who practice advertising, branding, direct marketing, graphic design, marketing, packaging, promotion, publicity, sponsorship, public relations, sales, sales promotion and online marketing are termed marketing communicators, marketing communication managers, or more briefly as marcom managers.

Traditionally, marketing communication practitioners focus on the creation and execution of printed marketing collateral; however, academic and professional research developed the practice to use strategic elements of branding and marketing in order to ensure consistency of message delivery throughout an organization - the same "look ' feel".

Strategy

A Strategy is a plan of action designed to achieve a particular goal.

Strategy is different from tactics. In military terms, tactics is concerned with the conduct of an engagement while Strategy is concerned with how different engagements are linked.

Lee

Lee is a brand of denim jeans, first produced in 1889 in Salina, Kansas. The company is owned by VF Corporation, the largest apparel company in the world. Its headquarters are currently in Merriam near Kansas City, Kansas.

Point

In typography, a point is the smallest unit of measure, being a subdivision of the larger pica. It is commonly abbreviated as pt. The traditional printer"s point, from the era of hot metal typesetting and presswork, varied between 0.18 and 0.4 mm depending on various definitions of the foot.

Today, the traditional point has been supplanted by the desktop publishing point (also called the PostScript point), which has been rounded to an even 72 points to the inch (1 point = $^{127}/_{360}$ mm ≈ 0.353 mm).

Positioning

In marketing, positioning has come to mean the process by which marketers try to create an image or identity in the minds of their target market for its product, brand, or organization. It is the "relative competitive comparison" their product occupies in a given market as perceived by the target market.

Re-positioning involves changing the identity of a product, relative to the identity of competing products, in the collective minds of the target market.

Taco Bell

Taco Bell is a restaurant chain based in Irvine, California, specializing in Mexican-inspired fast food. It is a subsidiary of Yum! Brands. Most restaurants are located in North America, but there are also many in other countries.

Toy

A Toy is an object used in play. Toy s are usually associated with children and pets, but it is not unusual for adult humans and some non-domesticated animals to play with Toy s. Many items are manufactured to serve as Toy s, but goods, or (game-centric) services produced for other purposes can also be used as Toy s.

Mind control

Mind control (also referred to as brainwashing, coercive persuasion, and thought reform) refers to a broad range of psychological tactics thought to subvert an individual"s control of his or her own thinking, behavior, emotions).

Wal-Mart

Wal-Mart Stores, Inc. is an American public corporation that runs a chain of large, discount department stores. It is the world"s largest public corporation by revenue, according to the 2008 Fortune Global 500.

Product

When a product reaches the maturity stage of the product life cycle a company may choose to operate strategies to extend the life of the product. If the product is predicted to continue to be successful or an upgrade is soon to be released the company can use various methods to keep sales, else the product will be left as is to continue to the decline stage.

Examples of extension strategies are:

	· Discounted price · Increased advertising · Accessing another market abroad Another strategy is added value. This is a widely used extension strategy.
Leo Burnett	Leo Burnett (October 21, 1891 - June 7, 1971) was an advertising executive famous for creating such icons as the Jolly Green Giant, the Marlboro Man, Toucan Sam, Charlie the Tuna, Morris the Cat, the Pillsbury Doughboy, the 7up "Spot", and Tony the Tiger. Burnett was named by Time magazine as one of the 100 most influential people of the 20th century. Born in St. Johns, Michigan, he studied journalism at the University of Michigan.
Relationship marketing	relationship marketing is a form of marketing developed from direct response marketing campaigns conducted in the 1970"s and 1980"s which emphasizes customer retention and satisfaction, rather than a dominant focus on "point of sale" transactions. relationship marketing differs from other forms of marketing in that it recognizes the long term value to the firm of keeping customers, as opposed to direct or "Intrusion" marketing, which focuses upon acquisition of new clients by targeting majority demographics based upon prospective client lists. relationship marketing refers to long-term and mutually beneficial arrangement wherein both buyer and seller focus on value enhancement through the certain of more satisfying exchange.This approach attempts to transcend the simple purchase exchange process with customer to make more meaningful and richer contact by providing a more holistic, personalized purchase, and use orn consumption experience to create stronger ties.
Quality	Quality in business, engineering and manufacturing has a pragmatic interpretation as the non-inferiority or superiority of something. Quality is a perceptual, conditional and somewhat subjective attribute and may be understood differently by different people. Consumers may focus on the specification Quality of a product/service, or how it compares to competitors in the marketplace.
Consumer	Consumer is a broad label for any individuals or households that use goods and services generated within the economy. The concept of a Consumer is used in different contexts, so that the usage and significance of the term may vary. Typically when business people and economists talk of Consumers they are talking about person as Consumer, an aggregated commodity item with little individuality other than that expressed in the buy/not-buy decision.
Consumer Reports	Consumer Reports is an American magazine published monthly by Consumers Union. It publishes reviews and comparisons of consumer products and services based on reporting and results from its in-house testing laboratory. It also publishes cleaning and general buying guides.

Report

In writing, a report is a document characterized by information or other content reflective of inquiry or investigation, which is tailored to the context of a given situation and audience. The purpose of report s is usually to inform. However, report s may include persuasive elements, such as recommendations, suggestions, or other motivating conclusions that indicate possible future actions the report reader might take.

Spatial analysis

In statistics, spatial analysis or spatial statistics includes any of the formal techniques which study entities using their topological, geometric, many still in their early development, using different analytic approaches and applied in fields as diverse as astronomy, with its studies of the placement of galaxies in the cosmos, to chip fabrication engineering, with its use of "place and route" algorithms to build complex wiring structures. The phrase is often used in a more restricted sense to describe techniques applied to structures at the human scale, most notably in the analysis of geographic data.

Trade

trade is the voluntary exchange of goods, services, or both. trade is also called commerce. A mechanism that allows trade is called a market.

Word association

Word Association is a common word game involving an exchange of words that are associated together.

Once an original word has been chosen, usually randomly or arbitrarily, a player will find a word that they associate with it and make it known to all the players, usually by saying it aloud or writing it down as the next item on a list of words so far used. The next player must then do the same with this previous word.

Asset

In business and accounting, assets are economic resources owned by business or company. Anything tangible or intangible that one possesses, usually considered as applicable to the payment of one''s debts is considered an asset. Simplistically stated, assets are things of value that can be readily converted into cash (although cash itself is also considered an asset).

Trademark

A Trademark or trade mark is a distinctive sign or indicator used by an individual, business organization and to distinguish its products or services from those of other entities.

A Trademark is designated by the following symbols:

· â„¢ (for an unregistered Trademark that is, a mark used to promote or brand goods);
· â„ (for an unregistered service mark, that is, a mark used to promote or brand services); and
· Â® (for a registered Trademark)

A Trademark is a type of intellectual property, and typically a name, word, phrase, logo, symbol, design, image, or a combination of these elements. There is also a range of non-conventional Trademark s comprising marks which do not fall into these standard categories.

The owner of a registered Trademark may commence legal proceedings for Trademark infringement to prevent unauthorized use of that Trademark

Ray Kroc

Ray Kroc took over the (at the time) small-scale McDonald''s Corporation franchise in 1954 and built it into the most successful fast food operation in the world. Kroc was included in Time 100: The Most Important People of the Century, and amassed a $500 million fortune during his lifetime. He was also the owner of the San Diego Padres baseball team starting in 1974.

Competition

Co-operative competition is based upon promoting mutual survival - "everyone wins". Adam Smith"s "invisible hand" is a process where individuals compete to improve their level of happiness but compete in a cooperative manner through peaceful exchange and without violating other people. Cooperative competition focuses individuals/groups/organisms against the environment.

Competitive

competitiveness is a comparative concept of the ability and performance of a firm, sub-sector or country to sell and supply goods and/or services in a given market. Although widely used in economics and business management, the usefulness of the concept, particularly in the context of national competitiveness, is vigorously disputed by economists, such as Paul Krugman .

The term may also be applied to markets, where it is used to refer to the extent to which the market structure may be regarded as perfectly competitive.

Sears

Sears, Roebuck and Co., commonly known as Sears, is an American mid-range chain of international department stores, founded by Richard Warren Sears and Alvah Roebuck in the late 19th century.

From its mail order beginnings, the company grew to become the largest retailer in the United States by the mid-20th century, and its catalogs became famous. Competition and changes in the demographics of its customer base challenged the company after World War II as its rural and inner city strongholds shrank and the suburban markets grew.

Volvo

The Volvo Group is a Swedish supplier of commercial vehicles such as trucks, buses and construction equipment, drive systems for marine and industrial applications, aerospace components and financial services. Although Volvo was incorporated in 1915 as a subsidiary of AB SKF, a Swedish ball bearing manufacturer, the auto manufacturer was officially founded on 14 April 1927, when the first car rolled off the factory in Hisingen, Gothenburg.

Volvo means "I roll" in Latin , conjugated from "volvere" (cp the ball bearing producer SKF.)

Parity

parity is a concept of equality of status or functional equivalence. It has several different specific definitions.

· parity (physics), a symmetry property of physical quantities or processes under spatial inversion
· parity (mathematics), indicates whether a number is even or odd
· parity (medicine), the number of times a woman or female animal has given birth
· parity (charity), UK equal rights organisation
· parity (law), legal principle
· parity bit, sets the parity of transmitted data for the purpose of error detection
· Purchasing power parity, in economics, the exchange rate required to equalise the purchasing power of different currencies
· Interest rate parity, in finance, the notion that the differential in interest rates between two countries is equal to the differential between the forward exchange rate and the spot exchange rate
· Put-call parity, in financial mathematics, defines a relationship between the price of a European call option and a European put option
· parity (sports), an equal playing field for all participants, regardless of their economic circumstances
· Potty parity, equalization of waiting times for males and females in restroom queues
· A tactic in othello
· Grid parity of renewable energy "

Promotion

Promotion involves disseminating information about a product, product line, brand, or company. It is one of the four key aspects of the marketing mix. (The other three elements are product marketing, pricing, and distribution). P>Promotion is generally sub-divided into two parts:

· Above the line Promotion: Promotion in the media (e.g. TV, radio, newspapers, Internet and Mobile Phones) in which the advertiser pays an advertising agency to place the ad
· Below the line Promotion: All other Promotion. Much of this is intended to be subtle enough for the consumer to be unaware that Promotion is taking place. E.g. sponsorship, product placement, endorsements, sales Promotion, merchandising, direct mail, personal selling, public relations, trade shows

Sale

A sale is the pinnacle activity involved in selling products or services in return for money or other compensation. It is an act of completion of a commercial activity.

A sale is completed by the seller, the owner of the goods.

Sales promotion

Sales promotion is one of the four aspects of promotional mix. (The other three parts of the promotional mix are advertising, personal selling, and publicity/public relations.) Media and non-media marketing communication are employed for a pre-determined, limited time to increase consumer demand, stimulate market demand or improve product availability.

Market Development

A Market development strategy targets non-buying customers in currently targeted segments. It also targets new customers in new segments. (Winer)

A marketing manager has to think about the following questions before implementing a Market development strategy: Is it profitable? Will it require the introduction of new or modified products? Is the customer and channel well enough researched and understood?

The marketing manager uses these four groups to give more focus to the market segment decision: existing customers, competitor customers, non-buying in current segments, new segments.

Research

research is defined as human activity based on intellectual application in the investigation of matter. The primary purpose for applied research is discovering, interpreting, and the development of methods and systems for the advancement of human knowledge on a wide variety of scientific matters of our world and the universe. research can use the scientific method, but need not do so.

Taco Bell

Taco Bell is a restaurant chain based in Irvine, California, specializing in Mexican-inspired fast food. It is a subsidiary of Yum! Brands. Most restaurants are located in North America, but there are also many in other countries.

Strategy

A Strategy is a plan of action designed to achieve a particular goal.

Strategy is different from tactics. In military terms, tactics is concerned with the conduct of an engagement while Strategy is concerned with how different engagements are linked.

Point

In typography, a point is the smallest unit of measure, being a subdivision of the larger pica. It is commonly abbreviated as pt. The traditional printer''s point, from the era of hot metal typesetting and presswork, varied between 0.18 and 0.4 mm depending on various definitions of the foot.

Today, the traditional point has been supplanted by the desktop publishing point (also called the PostScript point), which has been rounded to an even 72 points to the inch (1 point = $^{127}/_{360}$ mm ≈ 0.353 mm).

Competitive

competitiveness is a comparative concept of the ability and performance of a firm, sub-sector or country to sell and supply goods and/or services in a given market. Although widely used in economics and business management, the usefulness of the concept, particularly in the context of national competitiveness, is vigorously disputed by economists, such as Paul Krugman .

The term may also be applied to markets, where it is used to refer to the extent to which the market structure may be regarded as perfectly competitive.

Report

In writing, a report is a document characterized by information or other content reflective of inquiry or investigation, which is tailored to the context of a given situation and audience. The purpose of report s is usually to inform. However, report s may include persuasive elements, such as recommendations, suggestions, or other motivating conclusions that indicate possible future actions the report reader might take.

Positioning

In marketing, positioning has come to mean the process by which marketers try to create an image or identity in the minds of their target market for its product, brand, or organization. It is the "relative competitive comparison" their product occupies in a given market as perceived by the target market.

Re-positioning involves changing the identity of a product, relative to the identity of competing products, in the collective minds of the target market.

Consumer

Consumer is a broad label for any individuals or households that use goods and services generated within the economy. The concept of a Consumer is used in different contexts, so that the usage and significance of the term may vary.

Typically when business people and economists talk of Consumers they are talking about person as Consumer, an aggregated commodity item with little individuality other than that expressed in the buy/not-buy decision.

Consumer Reports

Consumer Reports is an American magazine published monthly by Consumers Union. It publishes reviews and comparisons of consumer products and services based on reporting and results from its in-house testing laboratory. It also publishes cleaning and general buying guides.

Leo Burnett

Leo Burnett (October 21, 1891 - June 7, 1971) was an advertising executive famous for creating such icons as the Jolly Green Giant, the Marlboro Man, Toucan Sam, Charlie the Tuna, Morris the Cat, the Pillsbury Doughboy, the 7up "Spot", and Tony the Tiger.

Burnett was named by Time magazine as one of the 100 most influential people of the 20th century. Born in St. Johns, Michigan, he studied journalism at the University of Michigan.

Toy

A Toy is an object used in play. Toy s are usually associated with children and pets, but it is not unusual for adult humans and some non-domesticated animals to play with Toy s. Many items are manufactured to serve as Toy s, but goods, or (game-centric) services produced for other purposes can also be used as Toy s.

Verizon

Verizon Communications Inc. (NYSE: VZ) is an American broadband and telecommunications company and a component of the Dow Jones Industrial Average. It was formed in 2000 when Bell Atlantic, one of the Regional Bell Operating Companies, merged with GTE.

Wireless

wireless communication is the transfer of information over a distance without the use of electrical conductors or "wires". The distances involved may be short (a few meters as in television remote control) or long (thousands or millions of kilometers for radio communications.) When the context is clear, the term is often shortened to "wireless".

Slogan

A slogan is a memorable motto or phrase used in a political, commercial, religious and other context as a repetitive expression of an idea or purpose. The word slogan is derived from slogorn which was an Anglicisation of the Scottish and Irish Gaelic sluagh-ghairm (sluagh "army", "host" + gairm "cry".) slogan s vary from the written and the visual to the chanted and the vulgar.

Tagline

A Tagline is a variant of a branding slogan typically used in marketing materials and advertising. The idea behind the concept is to create a memorable phrase that will sum up the tone and premise of a brand or product (like a film), or to reinforce the audience''s memory of a product. Some Taglines are successful enough to warrant inclusion in popular culture.

Trade

trade is the voluntary exchange of goods, services, or both. trade is also called commerce. A mechanism that allows trade is called a market.

Celebrity branding

Celebrity branding is a type of branding, in which a celebrity uses his or her status in society to promote a product, service or charity. Celebrity branding can take several different forms, from a celebrity simply appearing in advertisements for a product, service or charity, to a celebrity attending PR events, creating his or her own line of products or services, and/or using his or her name as a brand. The most popular forms of celebrity brand lines are for clothing and fragrances.

Advertising Age

Advertising Age (or AdAge) is a magazine, delivering news, analysis and data on marketing and media. The magazine was started as a broadsheet newspaper in Chicago in 1930. Today, its content appears in a print weekly distributed around the world and on many electronic platforms, including: AdAge.com, daily e-mail newsletters called Ad Age Daily, Ad Age''s Mediaworks and Ad Age Digital; weekly newsletters such as Madison ' Vine (about branded entertainment) and Ad Age China; podcasts called Why It Matters and various videos. AdAge.com also features a bookstore and a number of blogs, some created by the publication''s editorial team, others, such as Small Agency Diary are created by members of the Ad Age community.

Procter ' Gamble

Procter is a surname, and may also refer to:

· Bryan Waller Procter (pseud. Barry Cornwall), English poet
· Goodwin Procter, American law firm
· Procter ' Gamble, consumer products multinational "

Advertising campaign

An Advertising campaign is a series of advertisement messages that share a single idea and theme which make up an integrated marketing communication (IMC). Advertising campaigns appear in different media across a specific time frame.

The critical part of making an Advertising campaign is determining a champion theme as it sets the tone for the individual advertisements and other forms of marketing communications that will be used.

Generic

generic is something that is general, common, unique, or selective.

· generic mood, a grammatical mood used to make generalized statements like Snow is white
· generic antecedents, referents in linguistic contexts, which are classes.
· generic role-playing game system, a framework that provides rule mechanics for any setting--world or environment or genre
· generic drug, a drug identified by its chemical name rather than its brand name

In computer programming:

· generic function, a computer programming entity made up of all methods having the same name
· generic programming, (e.g. Free Pascal, C++, Java and C# generics) a computer programming technique that allows one value to take different datatypes in a type-safe manner
· generic, a component of the GNU Compiler Collection.
· generic!Artemis, a computer virus

In mathematics:

· generic filter, a mathematical filter that satisfies certain properties.
· generic point, a special kind of point whose behavior reflects the behavior of a closed subset of an algebraic variety or scheme.
· generic property, a formal definition of a property shared by almost all objects of a certain type. (For example, almost all functions in a given class or almost all points in a given space).
· generic formalism, a mathematical framework to describe irreversible phenomena in thermodynamics

In business:

· generic brand, a brand for a product that does not have an associated brand or trademark other than the trading name of the business providing the product
· genericized trademark, a trademark that sometimes or usually replaces a common term in colloquial usage
· an ordinary language word which is not a registered trade name.
· Porter generic strategies, a category scheme of business strategies
· Semi-generic, a term used in the United States for certain wine designations that hold no legal meaning

In toponymy:

· the component of a place name that indicates the type of place. For example, in the names Santa Monica Boulevard and Mount Everest, the generics are Boulevard and Mount.

In zoology:

· anything pertaining to a genus.

In music:

· Album - generic Flipper
· The Nintendo cover-band The Advantage was originally called generic, and the band generic is occasionally mentioned in scribblings by members of the band or their labels.

Proposition

This article is about the term proposition in logic and philosophy; for other uses see proposition

In logic and philosophy, proposition refers to either (a) the "content" or "meaning" of a meaningful declarative sentence or (b) the pattern of symbols, marks, or sounds that make up a meaningful declarative sentence. Propositions in either case are intended to be truth-bearers, that is, they are either true or false.

The existence of propositions in the former sense, as well as the existence of "meanings", is disputed by some philosophers.

Unique selling proposition

The Unique selling proposition is a marketing concept that was first proposed as a theory to explain a pattern among successful advertising campaigns of the early 1940s. It states that such campaigns made unique propositions to the customer and that this convinced them to switch brands. The term was invented by Rosser Reeves of Ted Bates ' Company.

Product

When a product reaches the maturity stage of the product life cycle a company may choose to operate strategies to extend the life of the product. If the product is predicted to continue to be successful or an upgrade is soon to be released the company can use various methods to keep sales, else the product will be left as is to continue to the decline stage.

Examples of extension strategies are:

· Discounted price
· Increased advertising
· Accessing another market abroad

Another strategy is added value.

This is a widely used extension strategy.

FUBU

FUBU is a clothing company. It includes casual wear, sports wear, a suit collection, eyewear, belts, and shoes. The name is a backronym for "FUBU", indicating that the product line was produced by black Americans for a primarily black American market.

Media Strategy

media strategy, as used in the advertising industry, is concerned with how messages will be delivered to consumers. It involves: identifying the characteristics of the target audience, who should receive messages and defining the characteristics of the media that will be used for the delivery of the messages, with the intent being to influence the behaviour of the target audience pertinent to the initial brief. Examples of such strategies today have revolved around an Integrated Marketing Communications approach whereby multiple channels of media are used i.e. advertising, public relations, events, direct response media, etc.

Resonance	In physics, resonance is the tendency of a system to oscillate at larger amplitude at some frequencies than at others. These are known as the system"s resonant frequencies (frequencies). At these frequencies, even small periodic driving forces can produce large amplitude vibrations, because the system stores vibrational energy.
Twinkie	A Twinkie is a "Golden Sponge Cake with Creamy Filling" popular in the United States and elsewhere in North America. Introduced by natives, it is distributed by Hostess, which is owned by Dallas-based Interstate Bakeries Corporation. Twinkies are the brainchild of James A. Dewar, one of Continental"s bakers. Realizing that several machines used to make cream-filled strawberry shortcake sat idle when strawberries were out of season, Dewar conceived a snack cake filled with banana cream, which would be dubbed the Twinkie.
Dangerous goods	dangerous goods,), are solids, liquids, other living organisms, property, or the environment. They are often subject to chemical regulations. dangerous goods include materials that are radioactive, flammable, explosive or corrosive, oxidizers or asphyxiants, biohazardous, toxic, pathogen or allergen substances and organisms.
Laddering	Laddering is an investment technique that requires investors to purchase multiple financial products with different maturity dates. Laddering avoids the risk of reinvesting a big portion of assets in an unfavorable financial environment. For example, a person has both a 2015 matured CD and a 2018 matured CD. Even if the interest rate drops fairly low in 2015 when one certificate is to be renewed, half of the income is locked in until 2018.
Sony	Sony Corporation is a multinational conglomerate corporation headquartered in Minato, Tokyo, Japan, and one of the world"s largest media conglomerates with revenue exceeding US$99.1 billion . Sony is one of the leading manufacturers of electronics, video, communications, video game consoles, and information technology products for the consumer and professional markets. Sony Corporation is the electronics business unit and the parent company of the Sony Group, which is engaged in business through its five operating segments--electronics, games, entertainment (motion pictures and music), financial services and other.
Department Store	A Department store is a retail establishment which specializes in satisfying a wide range of the consumer"s personal and residential durable goods product needs; and at the same time offering the consumer a choice multiple merchandise lines, at variable price points, in all product categories. Department stores usually sell products including apparel, furniture, home appliances, electronics, and additionally select other lines of products such as paint, hardware, toiletries, cosmetics, photographic equipment, jewelery, toys, and sporting goods. Certain Department stores are further classified as discount Department stores.
Walt Disney	Walter Elias "Walt" Disney (December 5, 1901 - December 15, 1966) was an American film producer, director, screenwriter, voice actor, animator, entrepreneur, entertainer, international icon and philanthropist. Disney is famous for his influence in the field of entertainment during the twentieth century. As the co-founder (with his brother Roy O. Disney) of Walt Disney Productions, Disney became one of the best-known motion picture producers in the world.
Copywriting	

Most copywriters are employees within organizations such as advertising agencies, public relations firms, web developers, company advertising departments, large stores, marketing firms, broadcasters and cable providers, newspapers, book publishers and magazines. Copywriters can also be independent contractors freelancing for a variety of clients, at the clients'' offices or working from their own, or partners or employees in specialized copywriting agencies.
A copywriter usually works as part of a creative team.

Bean

Bean is a common name for large plant seeds of several genera of the family Fabaceae (alternately Leguminosae) used for human food or animal feed.

The whole young pods of Bean plants, if picked before the pods ripen and dry, can be tender enough to eat whole, whether cooked or raw. Thus the word ''green Beans'' means ''green'' in the sense of unripe (many are in fact, not green in color), as the Beans inside the pods of green Beans are too small to comprise a significant part of the cooked fruit.

Volkswagen

The Volkswagen Automobile Company is an automobile manufacturer based in Wolfsburg, Germany, and is the original brand within the Volkswagen Group, as well as the largest brand by sales volume.

Volkswagen means ''people''s car'' in German, in which it is pronounced . Its current tagline or slogan is Das Auto .

Communication planning	communication planning is the art and science of reaching target audiences using marketing communication channels such as advertising, public relations, experiences or direct mail for example. It is concerned with deciding who to target, when, with what message and how. The Communication Plan serves as a guide to the communication and sponsorship efforts throughout the duration of the project.
Research	research is defined as human activity based on intellectual application in the investigation of matter. The primary purpose for applied research is discovering, interpreting, and the development of methods and systems for the advancement of human knowledge on a wide variety of scientific matters of our world and the universe. research can use the scientific method, but need not do so.
Taco Bell	Taco Bell is a restaurant chain based in Irvine, California, specializing in Mexican-inspired fast food. It is a subsidiary of Yum! Brands. Most restaurants are located in North America, but there are also many in other countries.
Media strategy	media strategy, as used in the advertising industry, is concerned with how messages will be delivered to consumers. It involves: identifying the characteristics of the target audience, who should receive messages and defining the characteristics of the media that will be used for the delivery of the messages, with the intent being to influence the behaviour of the target audience pertinent to the initial brief. Examples of such strategies today have revolved around an Integrated Marketing Communications approach whereby multiple channels of media are used i.e. advertising, public relations, events, direct response media, etc.
Target audience	In marketing and advertising, a target audience usually an advertising campaign, is aimed at appealing to. A target audience can be people of a certain age group, gender, marital status, etc. (ex: teenagers, females, single people, etc.)
Dangerous goods	dangerous goods,), are solids, liquids, other living organisms, property, or the environment. They are often subject to chemical regulations. dangerous goods include materials that are radioactive, flammable, explosive or corrosive, oxidizers or asphyxiants, biohazardous, toxic, pathogen or allergen substances and organisms.
Celebrity branding	Celebrity branding is a type of branding, in which a celebrity uses his or her status in society to promote a product, service or charity. Celebrity branding can take several different forms, from a celebrity simply appearing in advertisements for a product, service or charity, to a celebrity attending PR events, creating his or her own line of products or services, and/or using his or her name as a brand. The most popular forms of celebrity brand lines are for clothing and fragrances.
Sears	Sears, Roebuck and Co., commonly known as Sears, is an American mid-range chain of international department stores, founded by Richard Warren Sears and Alvah Roebuck in the late 19th century. From its mail order beginnings, the company grew to become the largest retailer in the United States by the mid-20th century, and its catalogs became famous. Competition and changes in the demographics of its customer base challenged the company after World War II as its rural and inner city strongholds shrank and the suburban markets grew.
Seasonality	In statistics, many time series exhibit cyclic variation known as seasonality, periodic variation, retail sales tend to peak for the Christmas season and then decline after the holidays.

Weight

In the physical sciences, the weight of an object is the magnitude, W, of the force that must be applied to an object in order to support it (i.e. hold it at rest) in a gravitational field. The weight of an object in static equilibrium equals the magnitude of the gravitational force acting on the object, less the effect of its buoyancy in any fluid in which it might be immersed. Near the surface of the Earth, the acceleration due to gravity is approximately constant; this means that an object''s weight near the surface of the Earth is roughly proportional to its mass.

Quantitative

A quantitative attribute is one that exists in a range of magnitudes, and can therefore be measured. Measurements of any particular quantitative property are expressed as a specific quantity, referred to as a unit, multiplied by a number. Examples of physical quantities are distance, mass, and time.

Frequency

Frequency is the number of occurrences of a repeating event per unit time. It is also referred to as temporal Frequency. The period is the duration of one cycle in a repeating event, so the period is the reciprocal of the Frequency.

Reach

In the application of statistics to advertising and media analysis, Reach refers to the total number of different people or households exposed, at least once, to a medium during a given period of time. Reach should not be confused with the number of people who will actually be exposed to and consume the advertising, though. It is just the number of people who are exposed to the medium and therefore have an opportunity to see or hear the ad or commercial.

Sale

A sale is the pinnacle activity involved in selling products or services in return for money or other compensation. It is an act of completion of a commercial activity.

A sale is completed by the seller, the owner of the goods.

Time

time is a component of the measuring system used to sequence events, to compare the durations of events and the intervals between them, and to quantify the motions of objects. time has been a major subject of religion, philosophy, and science, but defining time in a non-controversial manner applicable to all fields of study has consistently eluded the greatest scholars.

In physics and other sciences, time is considered one of the few fundamental quantities.

Consumer

Consumer is a broad label for any individuals or households that use goods and services generated within the economy. The concept of a Consumer is used in different contexts, so that the usage and significance of the term may vary.

Typically when business people and economists talk of Consumers they are talking about person as Consumer, an aggregated commodity item with little individuality other than that expressed in the buy/not-buy decision.

Consumer Reports

Consumer Reports is an American magazine published monthly by Consumers Union. It publishes reviews and comparisons of consumer products and services based on reporting and results from its in-house testing laboratory. It also publishes cleaning and general buying guides.

Procter ' Gamble

Procter is a surname, and may also refer to:

- Bryan Waller Procter (pseud. Barry Cornwall), English poet
- Goodwin Procter, American law firm
- Procter ' Gamble, consumer products multinational ''

Report

In writing, a report is a document characterized by information or other content reflective of inquiry or investigation, which is tailored to the context of a given situation and audience. The purpose of report s is usually to inform. However, report s may include persuasive elements, such as recommendations, suggestions, or other motivating conclusions that indicate possible future actions the report reader might take.

Availability

The most simple representation f is as a ratio of the expected value of the uptime of a system to the aggregate of the expected values of up and down time, or

$$A = \frac{E[\text{Uptime}]}{E[\text{Uptime}] + E[\text{Downtime}]}$$

If we define the status function X(t) as

$$X(t) = \begin{cases} 1, & \text{sys functions at time } t \\ 0, & \text{otherwise} \end{cases}$$

therefore, the availability is represented by

$$A(t) = \Pr[X(t) = 1].$$

$$E[X(t)] = X.\Pr[X(t) = 1] \quad t > 0.$$

Average availability must be defined on an interval of the real line. If we consider an arbitrary constant c, then average availability is represented as

$$A_c = \frac{1}{c}\int_0^c A(t)\,dt, \quad c > 0.$$

Limiting (or steady-state) availability is represented by

$$A = \lim_{t\to\infty} A(t).$$

Limiting average availability is also defined on an interval (0,c] as,

$$A_\infty = \lim_{c\to\infty} A_c = \lim_{c\to\infty} \frac{1}{c}\int_0^c A(t)\,dt, \quad c > 0.$$

availability is well established in the literature of stochastic modeling and optimal maintenance. Barlow and Proschan define availability of a repairable system as "the probability that the system is operating at a specified time t." While Blanchard gives a qualitative definition of availability as "a measure of the degree of a system which is in the operable and committable state at the start of mission when the mission is called for at an unknown random point in time." This definition comes from the MIL-STD-721. Lie, Hwang, and Tillman developed a complete survey along with a systematic classification of availability.

Competition

Co-operative competition is based upon promoting mutual survival - "everyone wins". Adam Smith"s "invisible hand" is a process where individuals compete to improve their level of happiness but compete in a cooperative manner through peaceful exchange and without violating other people. Cooperative competition focuses individuals/groups/organisms against the environment.

Goal

A Goal or objective is a projected state of affairs that a person or a system plans or intends to achieve--a personal or organizational desired end-point in some sort of assumed development. Many people endeavor to reach Goals within a finite time by setting deadlines.

A desire or an intention becomes a Goal if and only if one activates an action for achieving it .

Point

In typography, a point is the smallest unit of measure, being a subdivision of the larger pica. It is commonly abbreviated as pt. The traditional printer''s point, from the era of hot metal typesetting and presswork, varied between 0.18 and 0.4 mm depending on various definitions of the foot.

Today, the traditional point has been supplanted by the desktop publishing point (also called the PostScript point), which has been rounded to an even 72 points to the inch (1 point = $^{127}/_{360}$ mm ≈ 0.353 mm).

Psychographic

In the field of marketing, demographics, opinion research, and social research in general, psychographic variables are any attributes relating to personality, values, attitudes, interests, or lifestyles. They are also called IAO variables . They can be contrasted with demographic variables (such as age and gender), behavioral variables (such as usage rate or loyalty), and bizographic variables (such as industry, seniority and functional area.)

Selection

In the context of evolution, certain traits or alleles of a species may be subject to selection. Under selection, individuals with advantageous or "adaptive" traits tend to be more successful than their peers reproductively--meaning they contribute more offspring to the succeeding generation than others do. When these traits have a genetic basis, selection can increase the prevalence of those traits, because offspring will inherit those traits from their parents.

Television

television is a widely used telecommunication medium for transmitting and receiving moving images, either monochromatic ("black and white") or color, usually accompanied by sound. "television" may also refer specifically to a television set, television programming or television transmission.

Commercially available since the late 1930s, the television set has become a common communications receiver in homes, businesses and institutions, particularly as a source of entertainment and news.

Radio

radio is the transmission of signals by modulation of electromagnetic waves with frequencies below those of visible light. Electromagnetic radiation travels by means of oscillating electromagnetic fields that pass through the air and the vacuum of space. Information is carried by systematically changing some property of the radiated waves, such as amplitude, frequency, or phase.

Spatial analysis

In statistics, spatial analysis or spatial statistics includes any of the formal techniques which study entities using their topological, geometric, many still in their early development, using different analytic approaches and applied in fields as diverse as astronomy, with its studies of the placement of galaxies in the cosmos, to chip fabrication engineering, with its use of "place and route" algorithms to build complex wiring structures. The phrase is often used in a more restricted sense to describe techniques applied to structures at the human scale, most notably in the analysis of geographic data.

Competitive

competitiveness is a comparative concept of the ability and performance of a firm, sub-sector or country to sell and supply goods and/or services in a given market. Although widely used in economics and business management, the usefulness of the concept, particularly in the context of national competitiveness, is vigorously disputed by economists, such as Paul Krugman .

	The term may also be applied to markets, where it is used to refer to the extent to which the market structure may be regarded as perfectly competitive.
Co-operative competition	Co-operative competition is based upon promoting mutual survival - "everyone wins". Adam Smith''s "invisible hand" is a process where individuals compete to improve their level of happiness but compete in a cooperative manner through peaceful exchange and without violating other people. Cooperative competition focuses individuals/groups/organisms against the environment.
Mind control	Mind control (also referred to as brainwashing, coercive persuasion, and thought reform) refers to a broad range of psychological tactics thought to subvert an individual''s control of his or her own thinking, behavior, emotions).
King	The king is a playing card with a picture of a king on it. The usual rank of a king is as if it were a 13; that is, above the queen. In some games, the king is the highest-ranked card; in others, the ace is higher.
Vehicle	A Vehicle is a mechanical means of conveyance, a carriage or transport. Most often they are manufactured , although some other means of transport which are not made by humans also may be called Vehicles; examples include icebergs and floating tree trunks. Vehicles may be propelled or pulled by engines or animals including humans, for instance, a chariot, a stagecoach, a mule-drawn barge, an ox-cart or rickshaw.

Competitive

competitiveness is a comparative concept of the ability and performance of a firm, sub-sector or country to sell and supply goods and/or services in a given market. Although widely used in economics and business management, the usefulness of the concept, particularly in the context of national competitiveness, is vigorously disputed by economists, such as Paul Krugman .

The term may also be applied to markets, where it is used to refer to the extent to which the market structure may be regarded as perfectly competitive.

Marketing

marketing is a "social and managerial process by which individuals and groups obtain what they need and want through creating and exchanging products and values with others." It is an integrated process through which companies create value for customers and build strong customer relationships in order to capture value from customers in return.

marketing is used to create the customer, to keep the customer and to satisfy the customer. With the customer as the focus of its activities, it can be concluded that marketing management is one of the major components of business management.

Marketing Management

Marketing management is a business discipline which is focused on the practical application of marketing techniques and the management of a firm"s marketing resources and activities. Marketing managers are often responsible for influencing the level, timing, and composition of customer demand accepted definition of the term. In part, this is because the role of a marketing manager can vary significantly based on a business" size, corporate culture, and industry context.

Report

In writing, a report is a document characterized by information or other content reflective of inquiry or investigation, which is tailored to the context of a given situation and audience. The purpose of report s is usually to inform. However, report s may include persuasive elements, such as recommendations, suggestions, or other motivating conclusions that indicate possible future actions the report reader might take.

Sale

A sale is the pinnacle activity involved in selling products or services in return for money or other compensation. It is an act of completion of a commercial activity.

A sale is completed by the seller, the owner of the goods.

Taco Bell

Taco Bell is a restaurant chain based in Irvine, California, specializing in Mexican-inspired fast food. It is a subsidiary of Yum! Brands. Most restaurants are located in North America, but there are also many in other countries.

Role

A role or a social role is a set of connected behaviors, rights and obligations as conceptualized by actors in a social situation. It is an expected behavior in a given individual social status and social position. It is vital to both functionalist and interactionist understandings of society.

Switchers

The Switchers Trilogy is a fantasy book series for young adults, written by Kate Thompson. The series is mainly set in Ireland. The leading characters are teenagers with the power to shapeshift (or "Switch") into the forms of animals and various supernatural creatures.

· Tess: An only child who lives with her parents in Dublin city.

Target audience

In marketing and advertising, a target audience usually an advertising campaign, is aimed at appealing to. A target audience can be people of a certain age group, gender, marital status, etc. (ex: teenagers, females, single people, etc.)

Leo Burnett

Leo Burnett (October 21, 1891 - June 7, 1971) was an advertising executive famous for creating such icons as the Jolly Green Giant, the Marlboro Man, Toucan Sam, Charlie the Tuna, Morris the Cat, the Pillsbury Doughboy, the 7up "Spot", and Tony the Tiger.

Burnett was named by Time magazine as one of the 100 most influential people of the 20th century.

Born in St. Johns, Michigan, he studied journalism at the University of Michigan.

Toy

A Toy is an object used in play. Toy s are usually associated with children and pets, but it is not unusual for adult humans and some non-domesticated animals to play with Toy s. Many items are manufactured to serve as Toy s, but goods, or (game-centric) services produced for other purposes can also be used as Toy s.

Promotion

Promotion involves disseminating information about a product, product line, brand, or company. It is one of the four key aspects of the marketing mix. (The other three elements are product marketing, pricing, and distribution). P>Promotion is generally sub-divided into two parts:

· Above the line Promotion: Promotion in the media (e.g. TV, radio, newspapers, Internet and Mobile Phones) in which the advertiser pays an advertising agency to place the ad
· Below the line Promotion: All other Promotion. Much of this is intended to be subtle enough for the consumer to be unaware that Promotion is taking place. E.g. sponsorship, product placement, endorsements, sales Promotion, merchandising, direct mail, personal selling, public relations, trade shows

Trade

trade is the voluntary exchange of goods, services, or both. trade is also called commerce. A mechanism that allows trade is called a market.

Procter ' Gamble

Procter is a surname, and may also refer to:

· Bryan Waller Procter (pseud. Barry Cornwall), English poet
· Goodwin Procter, American law firm
· Procter ' Gamble, consumer products multinational "

Push

The business terms push and pull originated in the logistic and supply chain management, but are also widely used in marketing.

A push-pull-system in business describes the move of a product or information between two subjects. On markets the consumers usually "pulls" the goods or information they demand for their needs, while the offerers or suppliers "pushes" them toward the consumers.

Sampling	Sampling is that part of statistical practice concerned with the selection of individual observations intended to yield some knowledge about a population of concern, especially for the purposes of statistical inference. Each observation measures one or more properties (weight, location, etc.) of an observable entity enumerated to distinguish objects or individuals.
Strategy	A Strategy is a plan of action designed to achieve a particular goal. Strategy is different from tactics. In military terms, tactics is concerned with the conduct of an engagement while Strategy is concerned with how different engagements are linked.
Research	research is defined as human activity based on intellectual application in the investigation of matter. The primary purpose for applied research is discovering, interpreting, and the development of methods and systems for the advancement of human knowledge on a wide variety of scientific matters of our world and the universe. research can use the scientific method, but need not do so.
Celebrity branding	Celebrity branding is a type of branding, in which a celebrity uses his or her status in society to promote a product, service or charity. Celebrity branding can take several different forms, from a celebrity simply appearing in advertisements for a product, service or charity, to a celebrity attending PR events, creating his or her own line of products or services, and/or using his or her name as a brand. The most popular forms of celebrity brand lines are for clothing and fragrances.
Rebate	A Rebate is an amount paid by way of reduction, return, or refund on what has already been paid or contributed. It is a type of sales promotion marketers use primarily as incentives or supplements to product sales. The mail-in Rebate is the most common.
Consumer	Consumer is a broad label for any individuals or households that use goods and services generated within the economy. The concept of a Consumer is used in different contexts, so that the usage and significance of the term may vary. Typically when business people and economists talk of Consumers they are talking about person as Consumer, an aggregated commodity item with little individuality other than that expressed in the buy/not-buy decision.
Consumer Reports	Consumer Reports is an American magazine published monthly by Consumers Union. It publishes reviews and comparisons of consumer products and services based on reporting and results from its in-house testing laboratory. It also publishes cleaning and general buying guides.
Media Market	A Media market, broadcast market, media region, designated market area (DMA), Television Market Area (FCC term) or simply market is a region where the population can receive the same (or similar) television and radio station offerings, and may also include other types of media including newspapers and Internet content. They can coincide with metropolitan areas, though rural regions with few significant population centers can also be designated as markets. Conversely, very large metropolitan areas can sometimes be subdivided into multiple segments.

Sweepstakes	In the United States consumer sales promotions known as sweepstakes or simply sweeps (both single and plural) have become associated with marketing promotions targeted toward both generating enthusiasm and providing incentive reactions among customers by enticing consumers to submit free entries into drawings of chance (and not skill) that are tied to product or service awareness wherein the featured prizes are given away by sponsoring companies. Prizes can vary in value from less than one dollar to more than one million U.S. dollars and can be in the form of cash, cars, homes, electronics, etc. sweepstakes frequently have eligibility limited by international, national, state, local, or other geographical factors.
Competition	Co-operative competition is based upon promoting mutual survival - "everyone wins". Adam Smith"s "invisible hand" is a process where individuals compete to improve their level of happiness but compete in a cooperative manner through peaceful exchange and without violating other people. Cooperative competition focuses individuals/groups/organisms against the environment.
Walt Disney	Walter Elias "Walt" Disney (December 5, 1901 - December 15, 1966) was an American film producer, director, screenwriter, voice actor, animator, entrepreneur, entertainer, international icon and philanthropist. Disney is famous for his influence in the field of entertainment during the twentieth century. As the co-founder (with his brother Roy O. Disney) of Walt Disney Productions, Disney became one of the best-known motion picture producers in the world.
Free good	The free good is a term used in economics to describe a good that is not scarce. A free good is available in as great a quantity as desired with zero opportunity cost to society. A good that is made available at zero price is not necessarily a free good.
Incentive	In economics and sociology, an Incentive is any factor (financial or non-financial) that enables or motivates a particular course of action, the study of Incentive structures is central to the study of all economic activity (both in terms of individual decision-making and in terms of co-operation and competition within a larger institutional structure).
Merchandising	Merchandising is the methods, practices, and operations used to promote and sustain certain categories of commercial activity. In retail commerce, visual display Merchandising means maximizing merchandise sales using product design, selection, packaging, pricing, and display that stimulates consumers to spend more. This includes disciplines in pricing and discounting, physical presentation of products and displays, and the decisions about which products should be presented to which customers at what time.
Accounting profit	Accounting profit is the difference between price and the costs of bringing to market whatever it is that is accounted as an enterprise (whether by harvest, extraction, manufacture) in terms of the component costs of delivered goods and/or services and any operating or other expenses. A key difficulty in measuring profit is in defining costs. Pure economic monetary profits can be zero or negative even in competitive equilibrium when accounted monetized costs exceed monetized price.

Advertising Age

Advertising Age (or AdAge) is a magazine, delivering news, analysis and data on marketing and media. The magazine was started as a broadsheet newspaper in Chicago in 1930. Today, its content appears in a print weekly distributed around the world and on many electronic platforms, including: AdAge.com, daily e-mail newsletters called Ad Age Daily, Ad Age''s Mediaworks and Ad Age Digital; weekly newsletters such as Madison ' Vine (about branded entertainment) and Ad Age China; podcasts called Why It Matters and various videos. AdAge.com also features a bookstore and a number of blogs, some created by the publication''s editorial team, others, such as Small Agency Diary are created by members of the Ad Age community.

Cooperative

A cooperative (also co-operative or coöperative; often referred to as a co-op or coop) is defined by the International Co-operative Alliance''s Statement on the Co-operative Identity as an autonomous association of persons united voluntarily to meet their common economic, social, and cultural needs and aspirations through a jointly-owned and democratically-controlled enterprise. It is a business organization owned and operated by a group of individuals for their mutual benefit. A cooperative may also be defined as a business owned and controlled equally by the people who use its services or who work at it.

Public relations

public relations is the practice of managing the flow of information between an organization and its publics. public relations - often referred to as public relations - gains an organization or individual exposure to their audiences using topics of public interest and news items that do not require direct payment. Because public relations places exposure in credible third-party outlets, it offers a third-party legitimacy that advertising does not have.

Trade shows

A trade fair (trade show or expo) is an exhibition organized so that companies in a specific industry can showcase and demonstrate their latest products, service, study activities of rivals and examine recent trends and opportunities. Some trade fairs are open to the public, while others can only be attended by company representatives (members of the trade) and members of the press, therefore Trade shows are classified as either "Public" or "Trade Only". They are held on a continuing basis in virtually all markets and normally attract companies from around the globe.

Data migration

Data migration is the process of transferring data between storage types, formats, freeing up human resources from tedious tasks. It is required when organizations or individuals change computer systems or upgrade to new systems, or when systems merge (such as when the organizations that use them undergo a merger/takeover).

Database marketing

database marketing is a form of direct marketing using databases of customers or potential customers to generate personalized communications in order to promote a product or service for marketing purposes. The method of communication can be any addressable medium, as in direct marketing.

The distinction between direct and database marketing stems primarily from the attention paid to the analysis of data.

Direct marketing

Direct marketing is a sub-discipline and type of marketing. There are two main definitional characteristics which distinguish it from other types of marketing. The first is that it attempts to send its messages directly to consumers, without the use of intervening media.

Technology

Technology is a broad concept that deals with an animal species'' usage and knowledge of tools and crafts, and how it affects an animal species'' ability to control and adapt to its environment. Technology is a term with origins in the Greek "technologia", "τεχνολογÎÂ¯α" -- "techne", "τÎÂχνη" and "logia", "λογÎÂ¯α" ("saying".) However, a strict definition is elusive; "Technology" can refer to material objects of use to humanity, such as machines, hardware or utensils, but can also encompass broader themes, including systems, methods of organization, and techniques.

Telephone	The telephone is a telecommunications device that transmits and receives sound, most commonly the human voice. It is one of the most common household appliances in the developed world, and has long been considered indispensable to business, industry and government. The word telephone has been adapted to many languages and is widely recognized around the world.
Accountability	accountability is a concept in ethics with several meanings. It is often used synonymously with such concepts as responsibility, answerability, enforcement, blameworthiness, liability, and other terms associated with the expectation of account-giving. As an aspect of governance, it has been central to discussions related to problems in both the public and private (corporation) worlds.
FUBU	FUBU is a clothing company. It includes casual wear, sports wear, a suit collection, eyewear, belts, and shoes. The name is a backronym for "FUBU", indicating that the product line was produced by black Americans for a primarily black American market.
Sex	In biology, sex is a process of combining and mixing genetic traits, often resulting in the specialization of organisms into a male or female variety (known as a sex). sexual reproduction involves combining specialized cells (gametes) to form offspring that inherit traits from both parents. Gametes can be identical in form and function (known as isogametes), but in many cases an asymmetry has evolved such that two sex-specific types of gametes (heterogametes) exist: male gametes are small, motile, and optimized to transport their genetic information over a distance, while female gametes are large, non-motile and contain the nutrients necessary for the early development of the young organism.
Sex in advertising	Sex in advertising is the use of sexual or erotic imagery in advertising to draw interest to a particular product, for purpose of sale. A feature of Sex in advertising is that the imagery used, such as that of a pretty woman, typically has no connection to the product being advertised. The purpose of the imagery is to attract attention of the potential customer or user.
Time	time is a component of the measuring system used to sequence events, to compare the durations of events and the intervals between them, and to quantify the motions of objects. time has been a major subject of religion, philosophy, and science, but defining time in a non-controversial manner applicable to all fields of study has consistently eluded the greatest scholars. In physics and other sciences, time is considered one of the few fundamental quantities.
Copy platform	Plan for use by the copywriter that defines the basic theme of the advertising campaign and serves as a guide for writing an advertisement; , the Copy platform discusses the issues to be considered and describes the fundamental elements, such as slogans, visual symbols, and associations, to be built around the product (or service). It will also discuss the profile of the target audience, the product or service''s claims, the kinds of appeals to be used, the customer needs that the product or service will satisfy, and the image to be created, as well as the style, tone, and implications of the finished advertisement.
Copywriting	

Most copywriters are employees within organizations such as advertising agencies, public relations firms, web developers, company advertising departments, large stores, marketing firms, broadcasters and cable providers, newspapers, book publishers and magazines. Copywriters can also be independent contractors freelancing for a variety of clients, at the clients" offices or working from their own, or partners or employees in specialized copywriting agencies.

A copywriter usually works as part of a creative team.

File sharing

File sharing is the practice of distributing or providing access to digitally stored information, such as computer programs, multi-media (audio, video), documents, transmission, and distribution models. Common methods are manual sharing using removable media, centralized computer file server installations on computer networks, World Wide Web-based hyperlinked documents, and the use of distributed peer-to-peer (P2P) networking.

Infomercial

Infomercials are long-format television commercials, typically five minutes or longer. Infomercials are also known as paid programming (or teleshopping in Europe). This phenomenon started in the United States where Infomercials were typically shown overnight (usually 2:00 a.m. to 6:00 a.m).--outside of peak hours.

Telemarketing

telemarketing is a method of direct marketing in which a salesperson solicits to prospective customers to buy products or services, either over the phone or through a subsequent face to face or Web conferencing appointment scheduled during the call.

telemarketing can also include recorded sales pitches programmed to be played over the phone via automatic dialing. telemarketing has come under fire in recent years, being viewed as an annoyance by many.

Sales promotion

Sales promotion is one of the four aspects of promotional mix. (The other three parts of the promotional mix are advertising, personal selling, and publicity/public relations.) Media and non-media marketing communication are employed for a pre-determined, limited time to increase consumer demand, stimulate market demand or improve product availability.

Leo Burnett

Leo Burnett (October 21, 1891 - June 7, 1971) was an advertising executive famous for creating such icons as the Jolly Green Giant, the Marlboro Man, Toucan Sam, Charlie the Tuna, Morris the Cat, the Pillsbury Doughboy, the 7up "Spot", and Tony the Tiger.

Burnett was named by Time magazine as one of the 100 most influential people of the 20th century.

Born in St. Johns, Michigan, he studied journalism at the University of Michigan.

Taco Bell

Taco Bell is a restaurant chain based in Irvine, California, specializing in Mexican-inspired fast food. It is a subsidiary of Yum! Brands. Most restaurants are located in North America, but there are also many in other countries.

Celebrity branding

Celebrity branding is a type of branding, in which a celebrity uses his or her status in society to promote a product, service or charity. Celebrity branding can take several different forms, from a celebrity simply appearing in advertisements for a product, service or charity, to a celebrity attending PR events, creating his or her own line of products or services, and/or using his or her name as a brand. The most popular forms of celebrity brand lines are for clothing and fragrances.

Globalization

globalization (or globalisation) describes an ongoing process by which regional economies, societies, and cultures have become integrated through a globe-spanning network of communication and exchange. The term is sometimes used to refer specifically to economic globalization: the integration of national economies into the international economy through trade, foreign direct investment, capital flows, migration, and the spread of technology. However, globalization is usually recognized as being driven by a combination of economic, technological, sociocultural, political, and biological factors.

Marketing

marketing is a "social and managerial process by which individuals and groups obtain what they need and want through creating and exchanging products and values with others." It is an integrated process through which companies create value for customers and build strong customer relationships in order to capture value from customers in return.

marketing is used to create the customer, to keep the customer and to satisfy the customer. With the customer as the focus of its activities, it can be concluded that marketing management is one of the major components of business management.

Marketing communication

marketing communications (or MarCom or Integrated marketing communications) are messages and related media used to communicate with a market. Those who practice advertising, branding, direct marketing, graphic design, marketing, packaging, promotion, publicity, sponsorship, public relations, sales, sales promotion and online marketing are termed marketing communicators, marketing communication managers, or more briefly as marcom managers.

Traditionally, marketing communication practitioners focus on the creation and execution of printed marketing collateral; however, academic and professional research developed the practice to use strategic elements of branding and marketing in order to ensure consistency of message delivery throughout an organization - the same "look ' feel".

Product

When a product reaches the maturity stage of the product life cycle a company may choose to operate strategies to extend the life of the product. If the product is predicted to continue to be successful or an upgrade is soon to be released the company can use various methods to keep sales, else the product will be left as is to continue to the decline stage.

Examples of extension strategies are:

· Discounted price
· Increased advertising
· Accessing another market abroad

Another strategy is added value.

This is a widely used extension strategy.

Tiger

TIGER Referencing or TIGER/Line is a format used by the United States Census Bureau to describe land attributes such as roads, buildings, rivers, and lakes, as well as areas such as census tracts. TIGER was developed to support and improve the Bureau''s process of taking the Decennial Census.

The TIGER files do not contain the census demographic data, but merely the map data.

Procter ' Gamble

Procter is a surname, and may also refer to:

· Bryan Waller Procter (pseud. Barry Cornwall), English poet
· Goodwin Procter, American law firm
· Procter ' Gamble, consumer products multinational "

Demographic

Demographics data are selected population characteristics as used in government, marketing or opinion research). Commonly-used Demographics include sex, race, age, income, disabilities, mobility (in terms of travel time to work or number of vehicles available), educational attainment, home ownership, employment status, and even location.

Television

television is a widely used telecommunication medium for transmitting and receiving moving images, either monochromatic ("black and white") or color, usually accompanied by sound. "television" may also refer specifically to a television set, television programming or television transmission.

Commercially available since the late 1930s, the television set has become a common communications receiver in homes, businesses and institutions, particularly as a source of entertainment and news.

Market Development

A Market development strategy targets non-buying customers in currently targeted segments. It also targets new customers in new segments. (Winer)

A marketing manager has to think about the following questions before implementing a Market development strategy: Is it profitable? Will it require the introduction of new or modified products? Is the customer and channel well enough researched and understood?

The marketing manager uses these four groups to give more focus to the market segment decision: existing customers, competitor customers, non-buying in current segments, new segments.

Dangerous goods

dangerous goods,), are solids, liquids, other living organisms, property, or the environment. They are often subject to chemical regulations. dangerous goods include materials that are radioactive, flammable, explosive or corrosive, oxidizers or asphyxiants, biohazardous, toxic, pathogen or allergen substances and organisms.

Toy

A Toy is an object used in play. Toy s are usually associated with children and pets, but it is not unusual for adult humans and some non-domesticated animals to play with Toy s. Many items are manufactured to serve as Toy s, but goods, or (game-centric) services produced for other purposes can also be used as Toy s.

Relationship marketing	relationship marketing is a form of marketing developed from direct response marketing campaigns conducted in the 1970"s and 1980"s which emphasizes customer retention and satisfaction, rather than a dominant focus on "point of sale" transactions. relationship marketing differs from other forms of marketing in that it recognizes the long term value to the firm of keeping customers, as opposed to direct or "Intrusion" marketing, which focuses upon acquisition of new clients by targeting majority demographics based upon prospective client lists. relationship marketing refers to long-term and mutually beneficial arrangement wherein both buyer and seller focus on value enhancement through the certain of more satisfying exchange.This approach attempts to transcend the simple purchase exchange process with customer to make more meaningful and richer contact by providing a more holistic, personalized purchase, and use orn consumption experience to create stronger ties.
Walt Disney	Walter Elias "Walt" Disney (December 5, 1901 - December 15, 1966) was an American film producer, director, screenwriter, voice actor, animator, entrepreneur, entertainer, international icon and philanthropist. Disney is famous for his influence in the field of entertainment during the twentieth century. As the co-founder (with his brother Roy O. Disney) of Walt Disney Productions, Disney became one of the best-known motion picture producers in the world.
Federal Trade Commission	The Federal Trade Commission is an independent agency of the United States government, established in 1914 by the Federal Trade Commission Act. Its principal mission is the promotion of "consumer protection" and the elimination and prevention of what regulators perceive to be harmfully "anti-competitive" business practices, such as coercive monopoly. The Federal Trade Commission Act was one of President Wilson"s major acts against trusts.
Trade	trade is the voluntary exchange of goods, services, or both. trade is also called commerce. A mechanism that allows trade is called a market.
Activism	Activism, in a general sense, can be described as intentional action to bring about social change, political change, economic justice, or opposition to, one side of an often controversial argument. The word "Activism" is often used synonymously with protest or dissent, but Activism can stem from any number of political orientations and take a wide range of forms, from writing letters to newspapers or politicians, political campaigning, economic Activism (such as boycotts or preferentially patronizing preferred businesses), rallies, street marches, strikes, both work stoppages and hunger strikes, or even guerrilla tactics.
Green marketing	According to the American Marketing Association, Green marketing is the marketing of products that are presumed to be environmentally safe. Thus Green marketing incorporates a broad range of activities, including product modification, changes to the production process, packaging changes, as well as modifying advertising. Yet defining Green marketing is not a simple task where several meanings intersect and contradict each other; an example of this will be the existence of varying social, environmental and retail definitions attached to this term.
Promotion	Promotion involves disseminating information about a product, product line, brand, or company. It is one of the four key aspects of the marketing mix. (The other three elements are product marketing, pricing, and distribution). P>Promotion is generally sub-divided into two parts:

· Above the line Promotion: Promotion in the media (e.g. TV, radio, newspapers, Internet and Mobile Phones) in which the advertiser pays an advertising agency to place the ad
· Below the line Promotion: All other Promotion. Much of this is intended to be subtle enough for the consumer to be unaware that Promotion is taking place. E.g. sponsorship, product placement, endorsements, sales Promotion, merchandising, direct mail, personal selling, public relations, trade shows

Competitive

competitiveness is a comparative concept of the ability and performance of a firm, sub-sector or country to sell and supply goods and/or services in a given market. Although widely used in economics and business management, the usefulness of the concept, particularly in the context of national competitiveness, is vigorously disputed by economists, such as Paul Krugman .

The term may also be applied to markets, where it is used to refer to the extent to which the market structure may be regarded as perfectly competitive.

Report

In writing, a report is a document characterized by information or other content reflective of inquiry or investigation, which is tailored to the context of a given situation and audience. The purpose of report s is usually to inform. However, report s may include persuasive elements, such as recommendations, suggestions, or other motivating conclusions that indicate possible future actions the report reader might take.

Boat trailer

A Boat trailer is a Trailer (vehicle) designed to launch, retrieve, carry and , boatyards, boat hauliers, boat dealers and boat builders. Generally this type of trailer is not used for storage of the boat.

Wal-Mart

Wal-Mart Stores, Inc. is an American public corporation that runs a chain of large, discount department stores. It is the world''s largest public corporation by revenue, according to the 2008 Fortune Global 500.

Marketing co-operation

A marketing co-operation or marketing cooperation is a partnership of at least two companies on the value chain level of marketing with the objective to tap the full potential of a market by bundling specific competences or resources. Other terms f are marketing alliance, marketing partnership, co-marketing, and cross-marketing.

marketing co-operations are sensible when the marketing goals of two companies can be combined with a concrete performance measure for the end consumer.

Cooperative

A cooperative (also co-operative or coöperative; often referred to as a co-op or coop) is defined by the International Co-operative Alliance''s Statement on the Co-operative Identity as an autonomous association of persons united voluntarily to meet their common economic, social, and cultural needs and aspirations through a jointly-owned and democratically-controlled enterprise. It is a business organization owned and operated by a group of individuals for their mutual benefit. A cooperative may also be defined as a business owned and controlled equally by the people who use its services or who work at it.

Stereotype

A stereotype is a commonly held public belief about specific social groups, based on some prior assumptions.

Bean

Bean is a common name for large plant seeds of several genera of the family Fabaceae (alternately Leguminosae) used for human food or animal feed.

The whole young pods of Bean plants, if picked before the pods ripen and dry, can be tender enough to eat whole, whether cooked or raw. Thus the word "green Beans" means "green" in the sense of unripe (many are in fact, not green in color), as the Beans inside the pods of green Beans are too small to comprise a significant part of the cooked fruit.

Branded entertainment

Branded entertainment, also known as branded content or advertainment, is an entertainment-based vehicle that is funded by and complementary to a brand''s marketing strategy. The purpose of a Branded entertainment program is to give a brand the opportunity to communicate its image to its target audience in an original way, by creating positive links between the brand and the program.

Anything you do outside of work, money spent on activities outside "necessary" is entertainment.

Digital

A Digital system is a data technology that uses discrete (discontinuous) values. By contrast, non-Digital (or analog) systems use a continuous range of values to represent information. Although Digital representations are discrete, the information represented can be either discrete, such as numbers, letters or icons, or continuous, such as sounds, images, and other measurements of continuous systems.

Loyalty marketing

loyalty marketing is an approach to marketing, based on strategic management, in which a company focuses on growing and retaining existing customers through incentives. Branding, product marketing and loyalty marketing all form part of the customer proposition - the subjective assessment by the customer of whether to purchase a brand or not based on the integrated combination of the value they receive from each of these marketing disciplines.

The discipline of customer loyalty marketing has been around for many years, but expansions from it merely being a model for conducting business to becoming a vehicle for marketing and advertising have made it omnipresent in consumer marketing organizations since the mid- to late-1990s.

Digital media receiver

A Digital media receiver or digital media adapter (DMA) is a home entertainment device that can connect to a home network to retrieve digital media files (such as music, pictures) from a personal computer or other media server and play them back on a home theater system or TV. The DLNA organisation refers to these devices as digital media renderers .

A Digital media receiver can connect to the home network using either a wireless (IEEE 802.11a, b, g, and n) or wired (Ethernet) connection. A Digital media receiver includes a user interface that allows users to navigate through their digital media library, search for, and play back media files.

Sears

Sears, Roebuck and Co., commonly known as Sears, is an American mid-range chain of international department stores, founded by Richard Warren Sears and Alvah Roebuck in the late 19th century.

From its mail order beginnings, the company grew to become the largest retailer in the United States by the mid-20th century, and its catalogs became famous. Competition and changes in the demographics of its customer base challenged the company after World War II as its rural and inner city strongholds shrank and the suburban markets grew.

Twinkie

A Twinkie is a "Golden Sponge Cake with Creamy Filling" popular in the United States and elsewhere in North America. Introduced by natives, it is distributed by Hostess, which is owned by Dallas-based Interstate Bakeries Corporation.

Twinkies are the brainchild of James A. Dewar, one of Continental''s bakers. Realizing that several machines used to make cream-filled strawberry shortcake sat idle when strawberries were out of season, Dewar conceived a snack cake filled with banana cream, which would be dubbed the Twinkie.

Media strategy	media strategy, as used in the advertising industry, is concerned with how messages will be delivered to consumers. It involves: identifying the characteristics of the target audience, who should receive messages and defining the characteristics of the media that will be used for the delivery of the messages, with the intent being to influence the behaviour of the target audience pertinent to the initial brief. Examples of such strategies today have revolved around an Integrated Marketing Communications approach whereby multiple channels of media are used i.e. advertising, public relations, events, direct response media, etc.
Levi Strauss ' Co.	Levi Strauss (February 26, 1829 - September 26, 1902) was a German-Jewish immigrant to the United States who founded the first company to manufacture blue jeans. His firm, Levi Strauss ' Co., began in 1853 in San Francisco, California. Levi Strauss was born Löb Strauss in Buttenheim, in the Franconian region of Bavaria, Germany, to Hirsch Strauss and his wife Rebecca (Haass) Strauss.
Behavioral targeting	Behavioral targeting or behavioural targeting is a technique used by online publishers and advertisers to increase the effectiveness of their campaigns. Behavioral targeting uses information collected on an individual''s web-browsing behavior, such as the pages they have visited or the searches they have made, to select which advertisements to display to that individual. Practitioners believe this helps them deliver their online advertisements to the users who are most likely to be interested.
Interactivity	In the fields of information science, communication, and industrial design, there is debate over the meaning of interactivity. In the "contingency view" of interactivity, there are three levels: Noninteractive, when a message is not related to previous messages; Reactive, when a message is related only to one immediately previous message; and Interactive, when a message is related to a number of previous messages and to the relationship between them. Human communication is the basic example of interactive communication which involves two different processes; human to human interactivity and human to computer interactivity.
Consumer	Consumer is a broad label for any individuals or households that use goods and services generated within the economy. The concept of a Consumer is used in different contexts, so that the usage and significance of the term may vary. Typically when business people and economists talk of Consumers they are talking about person as Consumer, an aggregated commodity item with little individuality other than that expressed in the buy/not-buy decision.
Consumer Reports	Consumer Reports is an American magazine published monthly by Consumers Union. It publishes reviews and comparisons of consumer products and services based on reporting and results from its in-house testing laboratory. It also publishes cleaning and general buying guides.
Accountability	accountability is a concept in ethics with several meanings. It is often used synonymously with such concepts as responsibility, answerability, enforcement, blameworthiness, liability, and other terms associated with the expectation of account-giving. As an aspect of governance, it has been central to discussions related to problems in both the public and private (corporation) worlds.

Web banner	A web banner or banner ad is a form of advertising on the World Wide Web. This form of online advertising entails embedding an advertisement into a web page. It is intended to attract traffic to a website by linking to the website of the advertiser.
Research	research is defined as human activity based on intellectual application in the investigation of matter. The primary purpose for applied research is discovering, interpreting, and the development of methods and systems for the advancement of human knowledge on a wide variety of scientific matters of our world and the universe. research can use the scientific method, but need not do so.
Integrated Marketing Communications	integrated marketing communications is a term used to describe a holistic approach to marketing communication. It aims to ensure consistency of message and the complementary use of media. The concept includes online and offline marketing channels.
Guerrilla marketing	The concept of guerrilla marketing was invented as an unconventional system of promotions that relies on time, energy and imagination rather than a big marketing budget. Typically, guerrilla marketing campaigns are unexpected and unconventional; potentially interactive; and consumers are targeted in unexpected places. The objective of guerrilla marketing is to create a unique, engaging and thought-provoking concept to generate buzz, and consequently turn viral.
Sony	Sony Corporation is a multinational conglomerate corporation headquartered in Minato, Tokyo, Japan, and one of the world''s largest media conglomerates with revenue exceeding US$99.1 billion . Sony is one of the leading manufacturers of electronics, video, communications, video game consoles, and information technology products for the consumer and professional markets.
	Sony Corporation is the electronics business unit and the parent company of the Sony Group, which is engaged in business through its five operating segments--electronics, games, entertainment (motion pictures and music), financial services and other.
Undercover marketing	Undercover marketing (also known as buzz marketing, stealth marketing) is a subset of guerrilla marketing where consumers do not realize they are being marketed to. For example, a marketing company might pay an actor or socially adept person to use a certain product visibly and convincingly in locations where target consumers congregate. While there, the actor will also talk up their product to people they befriend in that location, even handing out samples if it is economically feasible.
Viral marketing	viral marketing and viral advertising refer to marketing techniques that use pre-existing social networks to produce increases in brand awareness or to achieve other marketing objectives (such as product sales) through self-replicating viral processes, analogous to the spread of pathological and computer viruses. It can be word-of-mouth delivered or enhanced by the network effects of the Internet. Viral promotions may take the form of video clips, interactive Flash games, advergames, ebooks, brandable software, images, or even text messages.
File sharing	File sharing is the practice of distributing or providing access to digitally stored information, such as computer programs, multi-media (audio, video), documents, transmission, and distribution models. Common methods are manual sharing using removable media, centralized computer file server installations on computer networks, World Wide Web-based hyperlinked documents, and the use of distributed peer-to-peer (P2P) networking.

Restaurant	A restaurant prepares and serves food and drink to customers. Meals are generally served and eaten on premises, but many restaurant s also offer take-out and food delivery services. restaurant s vary greatly in appearance and offerings, including a wide variety of cuisines and service models.
Ambush marketing	Ambush marketing is a marketing campaign that takes place around an event but does not involve payment of a sponsorship fee to the event. For most events of any significance, one brand will pay to become the exclusive and official sponsor of the event in a particular category or categories, and this exclusivity creates a problem for one or more other brands. Those other brands then find ways to promote themselves in connection with the same event, without paying the sponsorship fee and without breaking any laws.
	· 1984 Olympics; Kodak sponsors TV broadcasts of the Games as well as the US track team despite Fujifilm being the official sponsor. · 1988 Summer Olympics; Fujifilm sponsors the Games despite Kodak being the official sponsor. · 1992 Summer Olympics in Barcelona; Nike sponsors press conferences with the US basketball team despite Reebok being the official sponsor.
Telemarketing	telemarketing is a method of direct marketing in which a salesperson solicits to prospective customers to buy products or services, either over the phone or through a subsequent face to face or Web conferencing appointment scheduled during the call.
	telemarketing can also include recorded sales pitches programmed to be played over the phone via automatic dialing. telemarketing has come under fire in recent years, being viewed as an annoyance by many.

Research	research is defined as human activity based on intellectual application in the investigation of matter. The primary purpose for applied research is discovering, interpreting, and the development of methods and systems for the advancement of human knowledge on a wide variety of scientific matters of our world and the universe. research can use the scientific method, but need not do so.
Celebrity branding	Celebrity branding is a type of branding, in which a celebrity uses his or her status in society to promote a product, service or charity. Celebrity branding can take several different forms, from a celebrity simply appearing in advertisements for a product, service or charity, to a celebrity attending PR events, creating his or her own line of products or services, and/or using his or her name as a brand. The most popular forms of celebrity brand lines are for clothing and fragrances.
Integrated Marketing Communications	integrated marketing communications is a term used to describe a holistic approach to marketing communication. It aims to ensure consistency of message and the complementary use of media. The concept includes online and offline marketing channels.
Marketing	marketing is a "social and managerial process by which individuals and groups obtain what they need and want through creating and exchanging products and values with others." It is an integrated process through which companies create value for customers and build strong customer relationships in order to capture value from customers in return. marketing is used to create the customer, to keep the customer and to satisfy the customer. With the customer as the focus of its activities, it can be concluded that marketing management is one of the major components of business management.
Marketing Communication	marketing communications (or MarCom or Integrated marketing communications) are messages and related media used to communicate with a market. Those who practice advertising, branding, direct marketing, graphic design, marketing, packaging, promotion, publicity, sponsorship, public relations, sales, sales promotion and online marketing are termed marketing communicators, marketing communication managers, or more briefly as marcom managers. Traditionally, marketing communication practitioners focus on the creation and execution of printed marketing collateral; however, academic and professional research developed the practice to use strategic elements of branding and marketing in order to ensure consistency of message delivery throughout an organization - the same "look ' feel".
Promotion	Promotion involves disseminating information about a product, product line, brand, or company. It is one of the four key aspects of the marketing mix. (The other three elements are product marketing, pricing, and distribution). P>Promotion is generally sub-divided into two parts: · Above the line Promotion: Promotion in the media (e.g. TV, radio, newspapers, Internet and Mobile Phones) in which the advertiser pays an advertising agency to place the ad · Below the line Promotion: All other Promotion. Much of this is intended to be subtle enough for the consumer to be unaware that Promotion is taking place. E.g. sponsorship, product placement, endorsements, sales Promotion, merchandising, direct mail, personal selling, public relations, trade shows

Competitive

competitiveness is a comparative concept of the ability and performance of a firm, sub-sector or country to sell and supply goods and/or services in a given market. Although widely used in economics and business management, the usefulness of the concept, particularly in the context of national competitiveness, is vigorously disputed by economists, such as Paul Krugman .

The term may also be applied to markets, where it is used to refer to the extent to which the market structure may be regarded as perfectly competitive.

Report

In writing, a report is a document characterized by information or other content reflective of inquiry or investigation, which is tailored to the context of a given situation and audience. The purpose of report s is usually to inform. However, report s may include persuasive elements, such as recommendations, suggestions, or other motivating conclusions that indicate possible future actions the report reader might take.

Concept testing

Concept testing is the process of using quantitative methods and qualitative methods to evaluate consumer response to a product idea prior to the introduction of a product to the market. It can also be used to generate communication designed to alter consumer attitudes toward existing products. These methods involve the evaluation by consumers of product concepts having certain rational benefits, such as "a detergent that removes stains but is gentle on fabrics," or non-rational benefits, such as "a shampoo that lets you be yourself." Such methods are commonly referred to as Concept testing and have been performed using field surveys, personal interviews and focus groups, in combination with various quantitative methods, to generate and evaluate product concepts.

Competition

Co-operative competition is based upon promoting mutual survival - "everyone wins". Adam Smith"s "invisible hand" is a process where individuals compete to improve their level of happiness but compete in a cooperative manner through peaceful exchange and without violating other people. Cooperative competition focuses individuals/groups/organisms against the environment.

Department Store

A Department store is a retail establishment which specializes in satisfying a wide range of the consumer"s personal and residential durable goods product needs; and at the same time offering the consumer a choice multiple merchandise lines, at variable price points, in all product categories. Department stores usually sell products including apparel, furniture, home appliances, electronics, and additionally select other lines of products such as paint, hardware, toiletries, cosmetics, photographic equipment, jewelery, toys, and sporting goods. Certain Department stores are further classified as discount Department stores.

Procter ' Gamble

Procter is a surname, and may also refer to:

- Bryan Waller Procter (pseud. Barry Cornwall), English poet
- Goodwin Procter, American law firm
- Procter ' Gamble, consumer products multinational "

Copy platform

Plan for use by the copywriter that defines the basic theme of the advertising campaign and serves as a guide for writing an advertisement; , the Copy platform discusses the issues to be considered and describes the fundamental elements, such as slogans, visual symbols, and associations, to be built around the product (or service). It will also discuss the profile of the target audience, the product or service"s claims, the kinds of appeals to be used, the customer needs that the product or service will satisfy, and the image to be created, as well as the style, tone, and implications of the finished advertisement.

Copy testing
Copy testing is a specialized field of marketing research, it is the study of television commercials prior to airing them. It is defined as research to determine an ad"s effectiveness based on consumers" responses to the ad and covers all media including print, TV, radio, Internet etcAlthough also known as Copy testing, pre-testing is considered the more accurate, modern name (Young, p.4) for the prediction of how effectively an ad will perform, based on the analysis of feedback gathered from the target audience. Each test will either qualify the ad as strong enough to meet company action standards for airing or identify opportunities to improve the performance of the ad through editing.

Focus group
A Focus group is a form of qualitative research in which a group of people are asked about their attitude towards a product, service, concept, advertisement, idea, or packaging. Questions are asked in an interactive group setting where participants are free to talk with other group members.

The first Focus groups were created at the Bureau of Applied Social Research by associate director, sociologist Robert K. Merton.

Laddering
Laddering is an investment technique that requires investors to purchase multiple financial products with different maturity dates.

Laddering avoids the risk of reinvesting a big portion of assets in an unfavorable financial environment. For example, a person has both a 2015 matured CD and a 2018 matured CD. Even if the interest rate drops fairly low in 2015 when one certificate is to be renewed, half of the income is locked in until 2018.

Projective test
A Projective test in psychology, is a personality test designed to let a person respond to ambiguous stimuli, presumably revealing hidden emotions and internal conflicts. This is different from an "objective test" in which responses are analyzed according to a universal standard (for example, a multiple choice exam.) The responses to Projective test s are content analyzed for meaning rather than being based on presuppositions about meaning, as is the case with objective tests.

Questionnaire
A questionnaire is a research instrument consisting of a series of questions and other prompts for the purpose of gathering information from respondents. Although they are often designed for statistical analysis of the responses, this is not always the case. The questionnaire was invented by Sir Francis Galton.

SWOT analysis
SWOT analysis is a strategic planning method used to evaluate the Strengths, Weaknesses, Opportunities, and Threats involved in a project or in a business venture. It involves specifying the objective of the business venture or project and identifying the internal and external factors that are favorable and unfavorable to achieving that objective. The technique is credited to Albert Humphrey, who led a research project at Stanford University in the 1960s and 1970s using data from Fortune 500 companies.

Tachistoscope
A Tachistoscope is a device that displays (usually by projecting) an image for a specific amount of time. It can be used to increase recognition speed, to show something too fast to be consciously recognized, or to test which elements of an image are memorable. Actual Tachistoscopes use a slide or transparency projector equipped with the mechanical shutter system typical of a camera.

Likert scale
A Likert scale is a psychometric scale commonly used in questionnaires, and is the most widely used scale in survey research. When responding to a Likert questionnaire item, respondents specify their level of agreement to a statement. The scale is named after its inventor, psychologist Rensis Likert.

Market Research

market research is any organized effort to gather information about markets or customers. It is a very important component of business strategy. The term is commonly interchanged with marketing research; however, expert practitioners may wish to draw a distinction, in that marketing research is concerned specifically about marketing processes, while market research is concerned specifically with markets.

Television

television is a widely used telecommunication medium for transmitting and receiving moving images, either monochromatic ("black and white") or color, usually accompanied by sound. "television" may also refer specifically to a television set, television programming or television transmission.

Commercially available since the late 1930s, the television set has become a common communications receiver in homes, businesses and institutions, particularly as a source of entertainment and news.

Toy

A Toy is an object used in play. Toy s are usually associated with children and pets, but it is not unusual for adult humans and some non-domesticated animals to play with Toy s. Many items are manufactured to serve as Toy s, but goods, or (game-centric) services produced for other purposes can also be used as Toy s.

Product

When a product reaches the maturity stage of the product life cycle a company may choose to operate strategies to extend the life of the product. If the product is predicted to continue to be successful or an upgrade is soon to be released the company can use various methods to keep sales, else the product will be left as is to continue to the decline stage.

Examples of extension strategies are:

- Discounted price
- Increased advertising
- Accessing another market abroad

Another strategy is added value.

This is a widely used extension strategy.

Resources

Human beings are also considered to be Resources because they have the ability to change raw materials into valuable Resources. The term Human Resources can also be defined as the skills, energies, talents, abilities and knowledge that are used for the production of goods or the rendering of services. While taking into account human beings as Resources, the following things have to be kept in mind:

- The size of the population
- The capabilities of the individuals in that population

Many Resources cannot be consumed in their original form. They have to be processed in order to change them into more usable commodities.

Advertising campaign

An Advertising campaign is a series of advertisement messages that share a single idea and theme which make up an integrated marketing communication (IMC). Advertising campaigns appear in different media across a specific time frame.

The critical part of making an Advertising campaign is determining a champion theme as it sets the tone for the individual advertisements and other forms of marketing communications that will be used.

Audit

The general definition of an Audit is an evaluation of a person, organization, system, process, enterprise, project or product. Audits are performed to ascertain the validity and reliability of information; also to provide an assessment of a system''s internal control. The goal of an Audit is to express an opinion on the person / organization/system (etc) in question, under evaluation based on work done on a test basis.

Consumer

Consumer is a broad label for any individuals or households that use goods and services generated within the economy. The concept of a Consumer is used in different contexts, so that the usage and significance of the term may vary.

Typically when business people and economists talk of Consumers they are talking about person as Consumer, an aggregated commodity item with little individuality other than that expressed in the buy/not-buy decision.

Market analysis

A market analysis is a documented investigation of a Market that is used to inform a firm''s planning activities particularly around decision of: inventory, purchase, work force expansion/contraction, facility expansion, purchases of capital equipment, promotional activities, and many other aspects of a company.

Not all managers are asked to conduct a market analysis, but all managers must make decisions using market analysis data and understand how the data was derived. So all managers need a reasonable understanding of the tools most used for making sales forecasts and analyzing markets.

Situation analysis

Situation analysis is a marketing term, and involves evaluating the situation and trends in a particular company''s market. Situation analysis is often called the "three c''s", which refers to the three major elements that must be studied:

· Customers
· Costs
· Competition

The number of "c''s" is sometimes extended to four, five, or even six, with "Collaboration", "Company", and "Competitive advantage".

· Marketing mix
· SWOT analysis .

Technology

Technology is a broad concept that deals with an animal species'' usage and knowledge of tools and crafts, and how it affects an animal species'' ability to control and adapt to its environment. Technology is a term with origins in the Greek "technologia", "τεχνολογÎÂ¯α" -- "techne", "τÎÂχνη" and "logia", "λογÎÂ¯α" ("saying".) However, a strict definition is elusive; "Technology" can refer to material objects of use to humanity, such as machines, hardware or utensils, but can also encompass broader themes, including systems, methods of organization, and techniques.

Telephone

The telephone is a telecommunications device that transmits and receives sound, most commonly the human voice. It is one of the most common household appliances in the developed world, and has long been considered indispensable to business, industry and government. The word telephone has been adapted to many languages and is widely recognized around the world.

Gallup ' Robinson

Gallup ' Robinson is an independent marketing research firm specializing in advertising research. Founded in 1948, in Princeton, New Jersey by Dr. George Gallup and Dr. Claude Robinson, the company helps advertisers develop, evaluate and improve the effectiveness of their advertising in media.

The company has applied many of the research techniques introduced by both George Gallup and Claude Robinson, including measures of recall, profiled idea communication, voluntary reactions to advertising, persuasion and Day-After-Recall (DAR) techniques.

Sale

A sale is the pinnacle activity involved in selling products or services in return for money or other compensation. It is an act of completion of a commercial activity.

A sale is completed by the seller, the owner of the goods.

Celebrity branding

Celebrity branding is a type of branding, in which a celebrity uses his or her status in society to promote a product, service or charity. Celebrity branding can take several different forms, from a celebrity simply appearing in advertisements for a product, service or charity, to a celebrity attending PR events, creating his or her own line of products or services, and/or using his or her name as a brand. The most popular forms of celebrity brand lines are for clothing and fragrances.

Competition

Co-operative competition is based upon promoting mutual survival - "everyone wins". Adam Smith''s "invisible hand" is a process where individuals compete to improve their level of happiness but compete in a cooperative manner through peaceful exchange and without violating other people. Cooperative competition focuses individuals/groups/organisms against the environment.

Situation analysis

Situation analysis is a marketing term, and involves evaluating the situation and trends in a particular company''s market. Situation analysis is often called the "three c''s", which refers to the three major elements that must be studied:

· Customers
· Costs
· Competition

The number of "c''s" is sometimes extended to four, five, or even six, with "Collaboration", "Company", and "Competitive advantage".

· Marketing mix
· SWOT analysis .

Writing

writing is the representation of language in a textual medium through the use of a set of signs or symbols (known as a writing system.) It is distinguished from illustration, such as cave drawing and painting, and the recording of language via a non-textual medium such as magnetic tape audio.

In Eurasia writing began as a consequence of the burgeoning needs of accounting.

Market analysis

A market analysis is a documented investigation of a Market that is used to inform a firm''s planning activities particularly around decision of: inventory, purchase, work force expansion/contraction, facility expansion, purchases of capital equipment, promotional activities, and many other aspects of a company.

Not all managers are asked to conduct a market analysis, but all managers must make decisions using market analysis data and understand how the data was derived. So all managers need a reasonable understanding of the tools most used for making sales forecasts and analyzing markets.

Procter ' Gamble

Procter is a surname, and may also refer to:

· Bryan Waller Procter (pseud. Barry Cornwall), English poet
· Goodwin Procter, American law firm
· Procter ' Gamble, consumer products multinational "

Taco Bell

Taco Bell is a restaurant chain based in Irvine, California, specializing in Mexican-inspired fast food. It is a subsidiary of Yum! Brands. Most restaurants are located in North America, but there are also many in other countries.

Television	television is a widely used telecommunication medium for transmitting and receiving moving images, either monochromatic ("black and white") or color, usually accompanied by sound. "television" may also refer specifically to a television set, television programming or television transmission. Commercially available since the late 1930s, the television set has become a common communications receiver in homes, businesses and institutions, particularly as a source of entertainment and news.
Dangerous goods	dangerous goods,), are solids, liquids, other living organisms, property, or the environment. They are often subject to chemical regulations. dangerous goods include materials that are radioactive, flammable, explosive or corrosive, oxidizers or asphyxiants, biohazardous, toxic, pathogen or allergen substances and organisms.
SWOT analysis	SWOT analysis is a strategic planning method used to evaluate the Strengths, Weaknesses, Opportunities, and Threats involved in a project or in a business venture. It involves specifying the objective of the business venture or project and identifying the internal and external factors that are favorable and unfavorable to achieving that objective. The technique is credited to Albert Humphrey, who led a research project at Stanford University in the 1960s and 1970s using data from Fortune 500 companies.
Table	A table is both a mode of visual communication and a means of arranging data. The use of tables is pervasive throughout all communication, research and data analysis. Tables appear in print media, handwritten notes, computer software, architectural ornamentation, traffic signs and many other places.
Boat trailer	A Boat trailer is a Trailer (vehicle) designed to launch, retrieve, carry and , boatyards, boat hauliers, boat dealers and boat builders. Generally this type of trailer is not used for storage of the boat.

Competitive	competitiveness is a comparative concept of the ability and performance of a firm, sub-sector or country to sell and supply goods and/or services in a given market. Although widely used in economics and business management, the usefulness of the concept, particularly in the context of national competitiveness, is vigorously disputed by economists, such as Paul Krugman . The term may also be applied to markets, where it is used to refer to the extent to which the market structure may be regarded as perfectly competitive.
Report	In writing, a report is a document characterized by information or other content reflective of inquiry or investigation, which is tailored to the context of a given situation and audience. The purpose of report s is usually to inform. However, report s may include persuasive elements, such as recommendations, suggestions, or other motivating conclusions that indicate possible future actions the report reader might take.
Celebrity branding	Celebrity branding is a type of branding, in which a celebrity uses his or her status in society to promote a product, service or charity. Celebrity branding can take several different forms, from a celebrity simply appearing in advertisements for a product, service or charity, to a celebrity attending PR events, creating his or her own line of products or services, and/or using his or her name as a brand. The most popular forms of celebrity brand lines are for clothing and fragrances.
Competition	Co-operative competition is based upon promoting mutual survival - "everyone wins". Adam Smith"s "invisible hand" is a process where individuals compete to improve their level of happiness but compete in a cooperative manner through peaceful exchange and without violating other people. Cooperative competition focuses individuals/groups/organisms against the environment.
Consumer	Consumer is a broad label for any individuals or households that use goods and services generated within the economy. The concept of a Consumer is used in different contexts, so that the usage and significance of the term may vary. Typically when business people and economists talk of Consumers they are talking about person as Consumer, an aggregated commodity item with little individuality other than that expressed in the buy/not-buy decision.
Market analysis	A market analysis is a documented investigation of a Market that is used to inform a firm"s planning activities particularly around decision of: inventory, purchase, work force expansion/contraction, facility expansion, purchases of capital equipment, promotional activities, and many other aspects of a company. Not all managers are asked to conduct a market analysis, but all managers must make decisions using market analysis data and understand how the data was derived. So all managers need a reasonable understanding of the tools most used for making sales forecasts and analyzing markets.
Procter ' Gamble	Procter is a surname, and may also refer to: · Bryan Waller Procter (pseud. Barry Cornwall), English poet · Goodwin Procter, American law firm · Procter ' Gamble, consumer products multinational "

Product

When a product reaches the maturity stage of the product life cycle a company may choose to operate strategies to extend the life of the product. If the product is predicted to continue to be successful or an upgrade is soon to be released the company can use various methods to keep sales, else the product will be left as is to continue to the decline stage. Examples of extension strategies are:

· Discounted price
· Increased advertising
· Accessing another market abroad

Another strategy is added value.

This is a widely used extension strategy.

Taco Bell

Taco Bell is a restaurant chain based in Irvine, California, specializing in Mexican-inspired fast food. It is a subsidiary of Yum! Brands. Most restaurants are located in North America, but there are also many in other countries.

Target audience

In marketing and advertising, a target audience usually an advertising campaign, is aimed at appealing to. A target audience can be people of a certain age group, gender, marital status, etc. (ex: teenagers, females, single people, etc.)

Media strategy

media strategy, as used in the advertising industry, is concerned with how messages will be delivered to consumers. It involves: identifying the characteristics of the target audience, who should receive messages and defining the characteristics of the media that will be used for the delivery of the messages, with the intent being to influence the behaviour of the target audience pertinent to the initial brief. Examples of such strategies today have revolved around an Integrated Marketing Communications approach whereby multiple channels of media are used i.e. advertising, public relations, events, direct response media, etc.

Marketing

marketing is a "social and managerial process by which individuals and groups obtain what they need and want through creating and exchanging products and values with others." It is an integrated process through which companies create value for customers and build strong customer relationships in order to capture value from customers in return.

marketing is used to create the customer, to keep the customer and to satisfy the customer. With the customer as the focus of its activities, it can be concluded that marketing management is one of the major components of business management.

Marketing Management

Marketing management is a business discipline which is focused on the practical application of marketing techniques and the management of a firm"s marketing resources and activities. Marketing managers are often responsible for influencing the level, timing, and composition of customer demand accepted definition of the term. In part, this is because the role of a marketing manager can vary significantly based on a business" size, corporate culture, and industry context.

Sale

A sale is the pinnacle activity involved in selling products or services in return for money or other compensation. It is an act of completion of a commercial activity.

A sale is completed by the seller, the owner of the goods.

Direct marketing

Direct marketing is a sub-discipline and type of marketing. There are two main definitional characteristics which distinguish it from other types of marketing. The first is that it attempts to send its messages directly to consumers, without the use of intervening media.

Promotion

Promotion involves disseminating information about a product, product line, brand, or company. It is one of the four key aspects of the marketing mix. (The other three elements are product marketing, pricing, and distribution). P>Promotion is generally sub-divided into two parts:

· Above the line Promotion: Promotion in the media (e.g. TV, radio, newspapers, Internet and Mobile Phones) in which the advertiser pays an advertising agency to place the ad
· Below the line Promotion: All other Promotion. Much of this is intended to be subtle enough for the consumer to be unaware that Promotion is taking place. E.g. sponsorship, product placement, endorsements, sales Promotion, merchandising, direct mail, personal selling, public relations, trade shows

Public relations

public relations is the practice of managing the flow of information between an organization and its publics. public relations - often referred to as public relations - gains an organization or individual exposure to their audiences using topics of public interest and news items that do not require direct payment. Because public relations places exposure in credible third-party outlets, it offers a third-party legitimacy that advertising does not have.

Sales promotion

Sales promotion is one of the four aspects of promotional mix. (The other three parts of the promotional mix are advertising, personal selling, and publicity/public relations.) Media and non-media marketing communication are employed for a pre-determined, limited time to increase consumer demand, stimulate market demand or improve product availability.

Presenter

A presenter, in feminine form), is a person or organization responsible for running an event. A museum or university, for example, may be the presenter or host of an exhibit. Likewise, a master of ceremonies (also MC, emcee, or host) is a person that hosts or presents a show.

Writing

writing is the representation of language in a textual medium through the use of a set of signs or symbols (known as a writing system.) It is distinguished from illustration, such as cave drawing and painting, and the recording of language via a non-textual medium such as magnetic tape audio.

In Eurasia writing began as a consequence of the burgeoning needs of accounting.

Likert scale

A Likert scale is a psychometric scale commonly used in questionnaires, and is the most widely used scale in survey research. When responding to a Likert questionnaire item, respondents specify their level of agreement to a statement. The scale is named after its inventor, psychologist Rensis Likert.

SWOT analysis

SWOT analysis is a strategic planning method used to evaluate the Strengths, Weaknesses, Opportunities, and Threats involved in a project or in a business venture. It involves specifying the objective of the business venture or project and identifying the internal and external factors that are favorable and unfavorable to achieving that objective. The technique is credited to Albert Humphrey, who led a research project at Stanford University in the 1960s and 1970s using data from Fortune 500 companies.

Counter

In digital logic and computing, a Counter is a device which stores (and) the number of times a particular event or process has occurred, often in relationship to a clock signal. In practice, there are two types of Counters:

· up Counters, which increase (increment) in value
· down Counters, which decrease (decrement) in value

In electronics, Counters can be implemented quite easily using register-type circuits such as the flip-flop, and a wide variety of designs exist, e.g:

· Asynchronous (ripple) Counter - changing state bits are used as clocks to subsequent state flip-flops
· Synchronous Counter - all state bits change under control of a single clock
· Decade Counter - counts through ten states per stage
· Up-down Counter - counts both up and down, under command of a control input
· Ring Counter - formed by a shift register with feedback connection in a ring
· Johnson Counter - a twisted ring Counter
· Cascaded Counter

Each is useful for different applications. Usually, Counter circuits are digital in nature, and count in natural binary. Many types of Counter circuit are available as digital building blocks, for example a number of chips in the 4000 series implement different Counters.

Flowchart

A flowchart is a common type of diagram, that represents an algorithm or process, showing the steps as boxes of various kinds, and their order by connecting these with arrows. flowcharts are used in analyzing, designing, documenting or managing a process or program in various fields.

The first structured method for documenting process flow, the "flow process chart", was introduced by Frank Gilbreth to members of ASME in 1921 as the presentation "Process Charts--First Steps in Finding the One Best Way".

Table

A table is both a mode of visual communication and a means of arranging data. The use of tables is pervasive throughout all communication, research and data analysis. Tables appear in print media, handwritten notes, computer software, architectural ornamentation, traffic signs and many other places.

CPSIA information can be obtained at www.ICGtesting.com
Printed in the USA
BVOW050702310812

299281BV00001B/11/P

9 781428 842373